D0436185

THE ECCENTRIC
MR CHURCHILL

THE ECCENTRIC
MR CHURCHILL

LITTLE-KNOWN FACTS
ABOUT THE GREATEST BRITON

JACOB F. FIELD

Michael O'Mara Books Limited

First published in Great Britain in 2019 by
Michael O'Mara Books Limited
9 Lion Yard
Tremadoc Road
London SW4 7NQ

A CIP catalogue record for this book is available from the British Library.

Papers used by Michael O'Mara Books Limited are natural,
recyclable products made from wood grown in sustainable forests.
The manufacturing processes conform to the environmental
regulations of the country of origin.

ISBN: 978-1-78243-972-1 in hardback print format
ISBN: 978-1-78243-973-8 in ebook format

1 2 3 4 5 6 7 8 9 10

www.mombooks.com

Cover design by Claire Cater
Designed and typeset by Kay Hayden

Picture credits: p11 © Library of Congress, Prints and Photographs Division,
LC-USZ62-65636; p25 © Library of Congress, Prints and Photographs Division,
LC-USZ62-32833; p49 © Library of Congress, Prints and Photographs Division,
LC-USZ62-65632; p69 © Fox Photos / Getty Images; p87 © Globe Photos, Inc. /
ImageCollect; p99 © Mark Kauffman / The LIFE Picture Collection / Getty Images;
p111 © Library of Congress, Prints and Photographs Division, LC-USW33-019093;
p135 © Library of Congress, Prints and Photographs Division, LC-DIG-npcc-17934;
p143 © Globe Photos, Inc. / ImageCollect; p165 © Popperfoto / Getty Images; page
icons © Shutterstock

Every reasonable effort has been made to acknowledge all copyright holders. Any
errors or omissions that may have occurred are inadvertent, and anyone with any
copyright queries is invited to write to the publisher, so that full acknowledgement
may be included in subsequent editions of the work.

Printed and bound by CPI Group (UK) Ltd, Croydon, CR0 4YY

Contents

This one's for Ian and Pam

Introduction

Mr Churchill.

Or, if you are feeling a bit more formal: The Right Honourable Sir Winston Leonard Spencer-Churchill. Alternatively, one could try 'Prime Minister', 'First Lord of the Admiralty', 'Lord Warden of the Cinque Ports', 'Nobel Laureate', 'Chancellor of the Exchequer', 'Winnie', 'The British Bulldog', 'Lieutenant-Colonel Churchill', or just plain 'Pig'. Winston Churchill is known by many nicknames and titles – the last sobriquet was what his wife, Clementine Churchill, called him in private. For simplicity and brevity's sake, this book will simply refer to him by the initials he habitually used: WSC.

Perhaps no title is more fitting and deserved for WSC than 'The Greatest Briton of All', which he was given following a 2002 BBC poll that had over 1.5 million voters. WSC's status as the 'greatest Briton' was well earned, resting on his heroic leadership during the Second World War. In one of the darkest moments in British history, he provided hope and inspiration not just for his nation, but for everyone in the world who was fighting fascism. After becoming Prime Minister in 1940, WSC resisted all calls to make peace with Adolf Hitler, even when defeat seemed likely. Through his stirring rhetoric and astute leadership, he held together a nation that had been on the brink of being overwhelmed. In the cause of survival and victory he forged political alliances with people who had formerly been domestic rivals, such as the Labour leader Clement Attlee. On the international stage he travelled the world, by sea, land and air, in his desperate battle to hold together the Allies. This came at a great cost to his health (his war-time medical problems included a heart attack and pneumonia), but also stoked his ingenuity (WSC modified an oxygen mask so that he could smoke cigars at altitude). Despite the demanding conditions, he still insisted on his creature comforts, particularly in the dining room, as well as ensuring that his penchant for daily siestas and baths was met. During the war, WSC developed a close personal friendship with the American President Franklin D. Roosevelt (even though, as this book details, their first meeting, in 1918, had not gone well), while he also forged a more guarded working relationship with the Soviet leader Joseph Stalin (often lubricated with alcohol). Simply put, his tireless labours were essential in delivering Allied victory in 1945.

Although the Second World War was the zenith of WSC's lengthy career, it was illustrious and intriguing both before and after. For all his heroism, he was far more than a military leader. His life saw him journey across the world, come under fire on four continents, hold numerous political offices, become a best-selling author, and overcome setbacks both personal and professional. WSC had a multitude of interests and passions; he was endlessly curious and determined to live life to the full. In addition to his political and professional career, he was a famed raconteur and *bon vivant*, a style icon, a keen amateur sportsman and artist, as well as a loving husband and father. He was always constant to his essential self, a true one-off.

This book will uncover some of the lesser-known and fascinating features of WSC's life, and show that behind the 'greatest Briton' was a man who had an unconventional and original way of viewing the world, and a rugged determination to follow his beliefs and passions. From his preferred foods and drinks to his friends and enemies, from his daily routine in the Second World War to his favourite holiday destinations, it details the more obscure and eccentric moments, habits, hobbies and features that made WSC the man he was. So, settle down (possibly with a silver tankard of champagne – WSC would approve) and enjoy this intriguing celebration of an unparalleled life.

CHAPTER 1

The Early Years

THE DUKES OF MARLBOROUGH

WSC was a member of one of the most illustrious aristocratic families in England, the Spencer-Churchills. He directly descended from the famed general John Churchill, his great, great, great, great, great, great grandfather. Queen Anne awarded John Churchill the title of Duke of Marlborough in 1702 for his service as a general (during the 1930s WSC would write a four-volume biography of him). The family's seat was Blenheim Palace, built for them by the government between 1705 and 1722, which included 186 rooms set in seven acres of grounds. It was named in honour of the first duke's great victory over the French at the Battle of Blenheim (1704) in the War of the Spanish Succession.

The Dukes of Marlborough became the Spencer-Churchills as a result of the marriage of the first duke's daughter Anne to the statesman Charles Spencer, Earl of Sunderland. Their son Charles Spencer-Churchill became the third duke in 1733. WSC tended not to use his full surname, simply going by 'Churchill', although he would adopt 'S' as a middle initial. The Dukes of Marlborough were a central presence in English political life throughout the eighteenth and nineteenth centuries. WSC was the grandson of the seventh Duke of Marlborough, John Winston, a Conservative politician and minister. His father's older brother George inherited the duchy in 1883. WSC's cousin Charles, nicknamed 'Sunny' because one of his titles was the Earl of Sunderland, became the ninth duke in 1892. Until the birth of Sunny's son John in 1897, WSC was next in line to inherit the title.

LORD RANDOLPH

R andolph Churchill, WSC's father, was born on 13 February 1849 at 3 Wilton Terrace in Belgravia, London, to the seventh Duke of Marlborough and Lady Frances Anne Vane, the daughter of the Marquess of Londonderry, who had extensive estates in Ireland. As he was the second of their sons to survive into adulthood, he did not inherit the duchy. However, Randolph was allowed to use the courtesy prefix of 'Lord' (although he could not pass it on to his children). He attended Eton and matriculated at Merton College, Oxford, in 1867. Despite concentrating more on sport and drink-fuelled carousing (like Boris Johnson and David Cameron, he was a member of the Bullingdon Club), he graduated with a 2:1 in jurisprudence and modern history in 1870. Interested in politics from an early age, Randolph was elected as the Conservative MP for Woodstock in Oxfordshire in the February 1874 General Election.

JENNIE JEROME

W SC's mother, Jeanette (although she was always known as Jennie), was born in Brooklyn, New York, on 9 January 1854. Her father, Leonard Jerome, was a wealthy businessman who owned a majority share in *The New York Times*, several racehorses and an opera house, while her mother, Clara Hall, was the daughter of a landowner. Jennie's parents separated in 1867; happily, there was little acrimony and Leonard gave Clara enough income to allow her to move to Paris with Jennie and their two other surviving daughters, Clarita and Leonie. In Paris,

Jennie developed into a glamorous and charming sophisticate with striking good looks. Fluent in French and German, she was also a skilled pianist.

✌ The Tattooed Lady

Jennie Churchill had a small tattoo of a serpent on her left wrist, kept hidden by a bracelet she almost always wore.

RANDOLPH AND JENNIE

Cowes Week is a sailing regatta held every August off the Isle of Wight. The festival attracts thousands of wealthy and aristocratic visitors; in 1873 they included Randolph Churchill and Jennie Jerome. They first met at a reception and ball held on the HMS *Ariadne* to introduce members of the visiting Russian imperial family to High Society. Randolph and Jennie immediately hit it off; both were well travelled and keen horse riders. The next day Randolph came to dinner at the house where Jennie was staying with her mother and sisters. Jennie impressed Randolph with her expert piano-playing, and within days of meeting they were engaged.

Neither family was wildly enthusiastic about the match. Jennie's mother wanted someone of higher status for her daughter than the relatively impoverished second son of a duke, while Randolph's parents were not keen on their son marrying an American. Nonetheless, they began negotiating the marriage settlement. Disaster struck when Jennie's father withdrew his consent for the match in November 1873 when he found out the seventh Duke of

Marlborough was looking into his business affairs in New York. However, following a personal meeting with Randolph (and his successful election as an MP), he once more gave his consent to the union in February 1874. Jennie's dowry was £50,000 and the couple was given a joint annual income of £4,000. The wedding was celebrated at the chapel of the British embassy in Paris on 15 April. Following a European honeymoon and a brief period at Blenheim, they moved into a rented house in London's West End at 1 Curzon Street in Piccadilly.

THE BIRTH OF WINSTON

WSC was born at 1.30 a.m. on 30 November 1874 at Blenheim Palace. His parents had planned to have the birth at their home in London, but Jennie, so it is said, went into labour two months prematurely, during a visit to Blenheim. The baby was delivered after an eight-hour labour, overseen by Frederic Taylor, a local doctor. As WSC was born early, his parents had to borrow baby clothing from the wife of Mr Thomas Brown, a solicitor who lived near Blenheim. On 27 December WSC was baptized at the chapel in Blenheim, and named Winston after his paternal grandfather and Leonard for his maternal grandfather, who also stood as his godfather. His godmother was his paternal great-aunt Clementina, Marchioness Camden. In the new year, Randolph, Jennie and WSC returned to their London residence before moving to a new four-storey property at 48 Charles Street in Mayfair.

✌ Winston's First Nickname

WSC was a plump infant, so naturally he was nicknamed 'Skinny'.

'WOOMANY'

Like most upper-class Victorian parents, Randolph and Jennie mainly left child-rearing duties to hired help. Fortunately for Winston (and his younger brother Jack, born in 1880) their nanny, a Kentish woman called Mrs Elizabeth Ann Everest, was both capable and loving. The 'Mrs' was an honorific – she never married. WSC called her 'Old Woom' or 'Woomany', while she affectionately called him 'Winny'. When WSC left for school she continued to write to him about his health, even recommending heroin for toothache. She frequently travelled to tend WSC when he fell ill at boarding school, and attended speech day at Harrow with him instead of his parents. In 1891 Everest was moved on to join the staff of WSC's grandmother in London, but was abruptly fired after two years there. She eventually retired to live in Crouch End with her sister. Her health began to fail in the summer of 1895. WSC (now serving in the Army) rushed from his barracks in Aldershot to be with her. She died on 3 July with WSC by her side. He and Jack paid for and organized her funeral and tombstone. For the rest of his life WSC kept a photograph of her in his room.

A ROYAL SCANDAL

WSC's uncle George was married to Lady Albertha Hamilton, with whom he had four children. Until he inherited the title of Duke of Marlborough in 1883, George was known as the Marquess of Blandford. Around 1874, Blandford embarked on an affair with Edith, the wife of the Earl of Aylesford (also known as 'Sporting Joe'), having been introduced by the Prince of Wales. After Albertha found out about the affair, she left her husband. In November 1875, Aylesford joined the Prince of Wales on his tour of India, which gave Blandford the chance to get closer to Edith by moving into a hotel near her country house in Warwickshire. In early 1876, Edith wrote to her husband in India telling him she wished to elope with Blandford. When Aylesford returned to England he began divorce proceedings, naming Blandford as the co-respondent, blackening his name across London. To defend his brother's reputation Randolph leant on the Prince to force Aylesford to drop the suit, threatening to release racy, personal letters that the Prince had written to Edith. Incensed, the furious Prince was ready to duel Randolph in France, where the practice was still permitted. Queen Victoria called on Prime Minister Disraeli to calm the situation; he managed to get the families to reconcile, helped persuade Aylesford to drop the divorce case and had the incriminating letters burned. Disraeli then arranged for the seventh Duke of Marlborough to become Lord Lieutenant of Ireland. Randolph would act as his personal secretary, which meant he would have to reside in Dublin, removing him from London Society. He was joined by his wife, the two-year-old WSC and, of course, Mrs Everest.

LIFE IN IRELAND

The Churchills' Dublin home was the 'Little' White Lodge. It was situated in Phoenix Park, the estate that housed the official residence of the Lord Lieutenant. Although Randolph made frequent visits back to London (he was still a sitting MP), he developed an interest in Irish affairs and with Jennie visited all thirty-two counties. They also helped raise over £135,000 in charitable donations to a famine relief fund. WSC's first memories were of Ireland and were mostly fond, although in 1879 he fell off his donkey and was seriously concussed, leading to years of recurrent headaches. The Dublin interlude ended in March 1880, when Randolph had to return to England to prepare for the General Election. Although Randolph regained his Woodstock seat, his party lost power to the Liberals, leading to the appointment of a new Lord Lieutenant of Ireland. Now permanently returned to London, the Churchills settled in a new house at 29 St James's Place in Piccadilly before moving again in 1883 to 2 Connaught Place in Bayswater.

✌ Pocket Money

After Randolph was named Secretary of State for India in 1885, WSC made extra money by selling his father's signature to fellow students at Harrow. Later on, WSC also sold his mother's signature.

ST GEORGE'S SCHOOL

WSC was first sent to boarding school at the age of seven. He attended St George's School in Ascot, which was opened in 1877 and run by a cruel disciplinarian called Herbert Sneyd-Kynnersley. Sneyd-Kynnersley made liberal use of the cane, often giving boys twenty strokes for even small offences, usually drawing blood. Once he caned WSC for taking some sugar; in retaliation young Winston kicked the man's straw hat to pieces. Unsurprisingly, WSC despised St George's, where he was bottom of the class, and left in July 1884 following a bout of illness. In 1904 St George's became a girl's school, and it is still operating (in fact, Princess Beatrice of York attended from 2000 to 2007, and was Head Girl).

MOVING TO BRIGHTON

Following his unhappy time in Ascot, WSC was enrolled at a school in Brighton in September 1884, where he remained for nearly four years. Located near Hove, the school was run by two sisters called Kate and Charlotte Thomson. The sickly and asthmatic WSC was sent there on the recommendation of his doctor, Robson Roose, whose clinic was located nearby. In his early weeks there he found himself in trouble when, during a drawing examination, he got into an argument with another student about a knife they both needed. The quarrel ended with WSC being stabbed in the chest, leaving a quarter-inch-deep wound.

In March 1886, WSC suffered from a severe, possibly life-threatening, fever, when his temperature peaked at 104.3 degrees

Fahrenheit (40 degrees Celsius), but he was brought back to health following the ministrations of Dr Roose. Overall, WSC was much more content at the school, learning to swim, box and ride, enjoying his study of French, classics and history, and winning prizes for English and Scripture. He even trod the boards, playing Robin Hood in an opera put on at the school in 1887.

WINSTON THE HARROVIAN

WSC was sent to Harrow in April 1888 because he was thought to be not academic enough to attend Eton, his father's *alma mater*. His parents also believed that the air there would be better for WSC's constitution than the dampness of Thames-side Eton. His first essay at Harrow was on the subject of Palestine in the age of St John the Baptist. Ultimately, WSC's academic performance was never first-rate and he was initially placed in the bottom class of the school. He did, though, compose a poem titled 'The Influenza' (about an 1890 epidemic) that was published in the school magazine. WSC achieved highest prominence as a sportsman, becoming the Public Schools Fencing Champion in 1892. His style was fairly unorthodox and based on fleet movement and the element of surprise.

✌ A Prodigious Memory

One of WSC's greatest achievements at Harrow was his prodigious prize-winning feat of learning and reciting 1,200 lines from *Lays of Ancient Rome*, a collection of epic narrative poems by Thomas Babington Macaulay, published in 1842.

THE ROAD TO SANDHURST

A s a child WSC had a collection of 1,500 toy soldiers, which he loved to line up in formation. This passion for military matters helped persuade Randolph that the Army should be his oldest son's future career (this is a rather rose-tinted view; Randolph also believed his son was not bright enough to study law). At Harrow, WSC was relegated to the school's 'army class' in 1889 to prepare him to take the exam to enter the Royal Military Academy at Sandhurst in Norfolk. WSC failed in his first attempt at the entrance exam in August 1892, finishing 390th out of 693. He failed again in January 1893 so was sent to a 'crammer' in West London that specialized in getting boys into Sandhurst. He finally passed in August, receiving the news while on holiday in Switzerland. Unfortunately, he did not get enough marks to qualify for training as an infantry officer and was instead placed into the cavalry. This greatly annoyed Randolph, who wanted his son to enter an infantry regiment as it was cheaper than serving in the cavalry, where the extra kit and horses cost an additional £200 per annum. Happily, as a result of other candidates dropping out, WSC was ultimately offered a place in infantry training.

WSC started at Sandhurst in September 1893. He excelled in tactics and the study of fortifications, but won most renown for his horse riding. He passed out with honours in December 1894, finishing eighth in a class of 150. By lobbying Prince George, Duke of Cambridge, the commander-in-chief of the armed forces, Randolph had secured WSC a place in the prestigious 60th Rifles. Although this was a great opportunity, WSC was more attracted to the glamour of the cavalry, where promotions tended to be quicker and his small physique would be less of a problem. After

Randolph died in January 1895, Jennie charmed the Duke of Cambridge into letting WSC switch to the cavalry. He was to join the Fourth (Queen's Own) Hussars, a socially elite regiment based in Aldershot, scheduled to depart for India the next year, where adventure and glory would await.

A LOST WATCH

In July 1883 Randolph presented WSC with a gold watch that had belonged to the seventh Duke of Marlborough. The timepiece became a source of tension between them when WSC had to have it repaired after it was knocked out of his hand. In spring 1894, while at Sandhurst, WSC accidentally dropped it into a stream. After jumping into the cold water and failing to recover it, he hired twenty-three cadets, at a cost of £3, to make a dam and divert the water to drain the riverbed. It was recovered, but the repairs cost £3 17s, leading Randolph to give his son a new, cheaper watch.

✌ *Quid Pro Quo*, Winston

WSC never excelled at Latin and hated doing the translations he was set. By his final year at Harrow he had devised a scheme to get around it: a student more talented at classical languages would construe WSC's Latin; in return WSC would dictate his English essay to him.

FIRST PUBLIC SPEECH

WSC's illustrious career as a public speaker started in November 1894, shortly before he graduated from Sandhurst. It took place at the Empire Palace of Varieties in Leicester Square, the focus of the ire of pious anti-vice campaigners scandalized by its racy dancers and open promenade behind the dress circle where men and women could mingle and drink (to be fair to the critics, it *was* a noted haunt of prostitutes). When the time came to renew the Empire's licence, London County Council insisted that alcohol could not be served inside the auditorium, so canvas screens were set up between the promenade and the bars. The next Saturday, when WSC was attending the Empire, a crowd of around three hundred, incensed at the presence of the screens, tore them down. WSC was chief among their number, and had addressed them, urging them to bring down the screens to great cheers. In the long term their efforts were to no avail: the screens were eventually rebuilt in brick.

MONEY TROUBLES

In addition to his political career, Lord Randolph became a leading racehorse owner, but his primary investment was in South African goldfields, arranged by his friend the banker Nathaniel Rothschild. When Randolph died in 1895 his estate was worth £75,971. Unfortunately, most of this substantial amount (worth over £8 million today) was used to pay his debts, which included a £67,000 overdraft Randolph had run up at Rothschild's bank. The remainder went to a family trust administered by Jennie, giving her an annual income of £500. Under the terms of Randolph's will, the trust could be claimed by WSC and Jack if their mother remarried (as she did in 1900). However, she never informed them of this clause and continued to manage and benefit from the trust until her death. Furthermore, in 1898 Jennie persuaded WSC to sign away his £1,000 annual income from the trust to give her more cash to prop up her short-term debts.

CHAPTER 2

Friends and
Enemies

SUNNY AND CONSUELO

WSC's cousin Charles (nicknamed 'Sunny') was widely regarded as prickly and condescending. However, he was always close to WSC; they were childhood playmates, hunted together and both served in the Second Boer War. Sunny allowed WSC to stay at Blenheim Palace whenever he pleased and let him use his London bachelor flat at 105 Mount Street in Mayfair from 1901 to 1906.

When Sunny succeeded his father to become the ninth Duke of Marlborough in 1892, his family was in dire financial straits. He turned things around by marrying Consuelo Vanderbilt, an American heiress to a railroad empire, in 1895 (similarly, his father's second wife, Lily Warren Price, was another wealthy American whose money helped the family stay above water). Consuelo's dowry of $2.5 million (worth over £50 million today) and annual income of $100,000 effectively saved the duchy and paid for extensive restorations of Blenheim. Consuelo was a great beauty (literally so – she was six inches taller than her husband) and they had two sons (referred to as the 'heir and the spare'). Although Consuelo was always close to WSC, she grew to despise her husband, whom she had been forced to marry. They separated in 1906 and divorced in 1921. That same year, Consuelo married Jacques Balsan, a French aviator and balloonist, and remained with him until her death in 1964, at the age of eighty-seven.

Sunny likewise remarried in 1921, to his long-term mistress Gladys Deacon, an American socialite. Their relationship grew tempestuous, particularly after Sunny converted to Catholicism in 1927 (which WSC disapproved of); Gladys was said to have kept a revolver in her bedroom to prevent her husband entering. They eventually separated but had not yet divorced when Sunny died in 1934. Gladys's later life was tinged with tragedy: evicted from the duchy's properties she settled in Northamptonshire, becoming a recluse whose only human contact was with her Polish helper, Andrei Kwiatkowsky. In 1962 Gladys was forcibly removed to St Andrew's Hospital, a psychiatric institute in Northampton, where she died fifteen years later.

BROTHER JACK

B orn in Dublin on 4 February 1880, WSC's only brother was named John Strange Spencer-Churchill, soon shortened to 'Jack'. His unusual middle name came from a family friend John Strange Jocelyn, the Earl of Roden, an Irish peer rumoured to be his natural father. There was also gossip that Evelyn Boscawn, Viscount Falmouth or the Austrian nobleman Prince Karl of Kinsky (who later won the Grand National in 1883) might have a claim to Jack's paternity. Jack performed better academically than his older brother, and passed the exams for Harrow a year early, starting there in September 1892 and sharing a room with WSC. Jack distinguished himself with his impeccable behaviour, and set a record for not receiving a single punishment while a student at Harrow. He entered the Army in 1898, fighting in the Second Boer War alongside WSC. Without the independent income for a military career, Jack left the Army to work as a stockbroker, although he returned to his nation's service during the First World War, when he fought on the Western Front and in the Gallipoli Campaign, rising to the rank of major. Jack was good-natured and loyal, a steadfast and discreet supporter for WSC.

COUSIN CLARE

The daughter of WSC's maternal aunt Clara, Clare was born in 1885. After her husband Wilfred Sheridan died at the Battle of Loos in 1915, Clare moved to Paris to study sculpture. She was close to WSC until her support of the Bolshevik Revolution forced them apart. In 1920 Clare travelled to Moscow, where she produced busts of Lenin, Trotsky and other leading figures in the USSR. When she returned to England, she was publicly shunned and emigrated to the USA. She became a leading writer and journalist, interviewing the likes of Michael Collins, Benito Mussolini and Mustafa Kemal Atatürk. She had an affair with Charlie Chaplin and took part in an epic 4,000-mile motorcycle journey across Europe from England to the Black Sea port of Odessa. Eventually she and WSC put their differences aside and during the Second World War she made a sculpture of him at 10 Downing Street (he sat for it in bed with his Persian cat).

LEO AMERY AND SCHOOLBOY PRANKS

In his first year at Harrow, WSC pushed a fellow student into the swimming pond. The lad turned out to be a sixth former, head of house and champion of gymnastics called Leo Amery. He accepted WSC's apology and explanation: that he'd only pushed him in because he thought they were the same age on account of Amery's small stature. Later on, WSC's cheekiness to older boys led to a group of them seizing him and forcing him under a folded mattress while they poured hot and cold water on him. Amery became a Conservative MP, rising to become First Lord of the Admiralty and Secretary of State for the Colonies. In the parliamentary debate on the invasion of Norway in 1940, it was Amery who called on Neville Chamberlain to resign. This contributed to the Commons losing faith in Chamberlain's leadership, which directly led to WSC's rise to Prime Minister.

✌ The Prince of Wales

In 1887 WSC was formally introduced to the Prince of Wales (as well as his son, the future George V) on the royal yacht *Britannia* during the Golden Jubilee celebrations for Queen Victoria. That August the Prince presented both WSC and his brother Jack with gold tiepins set with diamonds. Their mother Jennie became the Prince's favourite mistress from 1896 to 1897. By then he had grown rather portly, so Jennie installed a lift to the bedroom in her London house for him. Two decades after their first meeting, the Prince, now reigning as Edward VII, gave WSC a gold-topped cane for his wedding.

LORD RANDOLPH: A DISTANT FATHER

WSC idolized his father Randolph – even though he was later to tell his own children that he'd never had more than five conversations with him – and felt he failed to live up to Randolph's expectations. Indeed, Randolph predicted WSC would be a wastrel with a 'shabby, unhappy and futile existence'.

Like many Victorians, Randolph placed a greater priority on his political career than on family life. He rose to prominence from 1880 as one of the 'Fourth Party' (a group of four backbench Conservative MPs that also included Henry Drummond Wolff, John Gorst and the future Prime Minister Arthur Balfour), which railed against the incumbent Liberals and the Tory establishment. Randolph was a proponent of 'Tory Democracy', which urged the party to adopt progressive reforms to appeal to the wider populace. He was an arch-critic of the Liberal leader William Gladstone, particularly his plans to give Ireland Home Rule, which Randolph remained a strident opponent of. When the Conservatives briefly returned to power from 1885 to 1886 in a caretaker ministry led by Lord Salisbury, Randolph was named Secretary of State for India. Even in this brief time, Randolph made his mark by authorizing the annexation of the last surviving part of the Kingdom of Burma. When Salisbury and the Conservatives returned to power following their victory in the July 1886 General Election, Randolph was appointed to the office of Chancellor of the Exchequer (which WSC later held from 1924 to 1929) as well as Leader of the House of Commons (because Salisbury sat in the House of Lords). Randolph's meteoric rise halted on 20 December, when he suddenly resigned as Chancellor over a dispute about military funding. He was swiftly replaced and never again held high office.

Randolph's health declined; he was a heavy drinker and chain-smoker and often worked himself to exhaustion. He was afflicted with heart palpitations and high blood pressure, as well as problems with hearing and speech. His medication made him moody and combative, and his speeches in the Commons were often rambling and incoherent. It is likely that he was suffering from late-stage syphilis, although alternative diagnoses such as a brain tumour or multiple sclerosis have also been suggested.

Despite this, from 1891 to 1892 Randolph spent months travelling through South Africa, splitting his time between hunting and gold-prospecting. In June 1894 Randolph embarked on a world tour with Jennie, hoping it would restore his health. They travelled through the USA and into Asia, but his illness forced them to return home peremptorily from Cairo in December. On Christmas Eve, Randolph and Jennie arrived in Dover, where they were met by WSC. Randolph was rushed to his mother's London residence in Grosvenor Square, where he died on 24 January 1895, having been in great pain for a month.

🖐 An American Mentor

William Bourke Cockran was an Irish-American lawyer and politician, considered one of the finest public speakers in the USA. He was introduced to Jennie in 1895 while they were both in Paris, and they had a brief affair. When WSC was in New York later that year, Bourke Cockran met him off the boat and toured him around the city. On WSC's next visit to New York, in 1900, Bourke Cockran introduced him to the President, William McKinley, at a dinner at the Waldorf Hotel. Bourke Cockran's eloquence made a great impression on WSC, and he credited him with being a major influence on his oratorical style.

THE WIDOW CHURCHILL

....

WSC adored his mother Jennie despite her constant affairs and spendthrift ways. After Lord Randolph died, Jennie purchased a seven-storey London townhouse at 35a Great Cumberland Place in Marylebone. It was grandly decorated (and included Jennie's beloved collection of crystal pigs) and had a staff of seven servants. Jennie embarked on a business enterprise, launching and editing a quarterly miscellany called *The Anglo-Saxon Review* (helped by WSC). Although its subscribers included royals, nobles and the wealthiest members of British and American society, the publication only ran from June 1899 to September 1901. Jennie also threw herself into charity work, and in 1899 raised over £40,000 to charter a hospital ship, the RFA *Maine*, to send to South Africa to care for wounded British soldiers serving in the Second Boer War.

In July 1900 Jennie married one of her lovers, George Cornwallis-West, a captain in the Scots Guards. Despite being just two weeks his senior, WSC tried to welcome Cornwallis-West into the family. Cornwallis-West's noble but impecunious family were dismayed that he had married an older woman with no great fortune and declined to attend the wedding. In 1905 the couple sold their London house and moved to Salisbury Hall near St Albans, the former home of Nell Gwynne, Charles II's mistress. Cornwallis-West made a series of bad investments and began to prefer fishing and the company of other women to his wife.

Jennie had a series of lovers and once again threw herself into charity work and another new venture: an elaborate Elizabethan pageant that she put on at Earl's Court in 1912. It featured actors dressed in period costume, a Tudor village, a replica of the Globe

Theatre and a life-sized model of Sir Francis Drake's galleon *Revenge*. One of the backers was a lover of Cornwallis-West, an American tin-plate heiress whom he persuaded to invest £15,000. Although it attracted publicity (George V and Queen Mary both visited), Jennie ran over budget and gave out excessive numbers of complimentary tickets to her friends. The pageant lost £50,000 – happily, the costs were not borne by Jennie herself but by her backers and investors. Jennie and Cornwallis-West divorced in 1914. Later that year he married the celebrated actress Stella Campbell before passing away in 1951.

After the First World War broke out Jennie embarked on more charity work, acting as a fundraiser for the American Women's War Relief Fund and as honorary head matron at a hospital for wounded officers in London and a convalescent home in Paignton, Devon. In 1918 Jennie married Montagu Porch, a soldier and colonial official three years younger than WSC. Sadly, in 1921 Jennie tripped down a set of stairs while wearing a new pair of shoes. This resulted in a fracture, gangrene and leg amputation, leading to her death from a haemorrhage on 29 June. Porch remarried an Italian noblewoman called Donna Guilia Patrizi. During the Second World War, he wrote to his stepson asking permission to keep his Italian manservant out of an internment camp; WSC complied with his request. Porch died in November 1964, a few months before his stepson.

FIRST LOVE

While WSC was serving in India in 1899, he met Pamela Plowden, the daughter of a senior colonial official. They grew close, enjoying an elephant ride together. He wrote her countless letters, presented her with the manuscript of his first (and only) novel, *Savrola*, and when he went to South Africa he carried three pictures of her in a special wallet. In October 1900, when they were both back in England, he proposed to her while punting on the River Avon beside Warwick Castle. Pamela rejected him and, two years later, married the Earl of Lytton. They had two sons; tragically, the eldest, Anthony, died in an air-crash in 1933 and the second, Alexander, died at the Battle of El Alamein in 1942. WSC, still loyal to his old flame, travelled to Hertfordshire to deliver the news to her in person.

STAGE BEAUTY

Ethel Barrymore was a leading American actress (and the great-aunt of Drew Barrymore). WSC saw her perform in 1901 in a one-night-only performance of the comedy *Captain Jinks of the Horse Marines* by Clyde Fitch. In 1902 and 1903 she visited Blenheim and regularly corresponded with WSC. In 1904 Barrymore returned to London to star in a production of *Cynthia* by Hubert Henry Davies at Wyndham's Theatre. While Ethel was rehearsing the play, WSC proposed to her, but she was uninterested. *Cynthia* closed after one disastrous performance and Ethel returned to the USA.

THIRD TIME'S THE CHARM? (NO)

Sir Arthur Wilson ran the world's largest privately owned steamship company. His daughter Muriel not only stood to inherit a huge fortune, but was also a noted beauty who starred in historical pageants and amateur theatrical productions (pictures of her in costume were a popular feature of contemporary society magazines). She was friends with WSC and tried to help him overcome his slight lisp by reciting the phrase, 'the Spanish ships I cannot see for they are not in sight'. However, she turned down his proposal in autumn 1904. Despite this, they holidayed in Italy together in September 1906, driving from Venice to Tuscany. Muriel was eventually married in 1917 to an army officer called Major Dick Warde.

THE POLITICAL MENTOR

David Lloyd George, 'The Welsh Wizard', was the leading figure of early-twentieth-century British politics and Prime Minister from 1916 to 1922. He first met WSC after he gave his maiden speech in the Commons in 1901. Even though they were then in opposing parties, Lloyd George complimented him. When WSC joined the Liberals in 1904, Lloyd George became his political mentor, and they frequently appeared together while campaigning. Despite WSC re-joining the Conservatives in 1924, they remained close throughout the 1930s, holidaying together in Morocco. When he became Prime Minister, WSC offered Lloyd George the post of ambassador to the USA, but he turned it down on grounds of ill health. They met for the last time in May 1944 in the Commons, the place where their friendship had begun. Lloyd George died of cancer less than a year later, and WSC delivered a heartfelt testimonial at his funeral.

THE PRIVATE SECRETARY

Edward Marsh was a friend of Pamela Plowden's and a clerk in the West African section of the Colonial Office. After meeting WSC several times, he became his private secretary in 1905. Marsh remained at his side until his first retirement from front-bench politics in 1929.

The civil service was just one side of Marsh's life; he was also a major figure in the British literary scene and a well-known member of London's gay community. In addition to editing WSC's writing, he was a proofreader for the likes of A. A. Milne and Somerset Maugham, as well as friends with Rupert Brooke, Ivor Novello and Siegfried Sassoon.

✌ The Knack of Napping

One of Edward Marsh's most useful skills was being able to sleep sitting up, as if deep in thought, and immediately wake up if roused. WSC copied this technique and used it to take brief naps to keep his energy levels up.

THE WIFE

Lady Blanche Ogilvy was the daughter of a Scottish peer, the Earl of Airlie. In 1873 she married Colonel Sir Henry Montague Hozier, a banker and former soldier (his distinguished military career included a period as British Assistant Military Attaché to German forces during the Franco-Prussian War, for which he was awarded the Iron Cross). Their second daughter, Clementine, was born in 1885. However, her paternity is a subject of debate, as Blanche's affairs were numerous and it was reported that Henry was sterile. As a result of Blanche's infidelities, her marriage broke up in 1891.

Clementine's family were not wealthy, and to make additional money she gave French lessons for half a crown per hour (about £12 today). She met WSC briefly in 1904, but at the time he was more interested in pursuing the likes of Ethel Barrymore and Muriel Wilson. They met again in March 1908 at a dinner party hosted by Clementine's aunt. WSC was enraptured and the feeling was mutual. After exchanging several letters, Clementine received an invitation from WSC's cousin Sunny to stay at Blenheim Palace. The invitation had been sent out at WSC's behest; he planned to propose but, perhaps because of an uncharacteristic bout of nerves, for three days he did not. Spurred into action by his cousin, on 12 August WSC proposed to Clementine in the formal gardens.

They married on 12 September 1908 at St Margaret's Westminster. Their union lasted over half a century, during which time 'Clemmie' was the rock upon which WSC's great achievements were built.

THE SPURNED WOMAN

The Liberal H. H. Asquith was the Prime Minister from 1908 to 1916. His daughter Violet was educated, opinionated and politically active. She first met WSC, over twelve years her senior, at a dinner party in 1906 and they grew close over the next two years. Much to her chagrin, WSC instead proposed to Clemmie (who Violet described as 'stupid as an owl'). After the proposal, WSC holidayed with Violet at New Slains Castle on the Aberdeenshire coast so that he could explain his decision face to face. The next month (the week after WSC and Clemmie's wedding day) Violet went missing, leading to a huge search. It was feared she had been swept away into the sea until she was found uninjured on a ledge. She claimed she had slipped and hit her head, but it may have been a bid to gain attention.

In 1915 Violet married Sir Maurice Bonham Carter, her father's Principal Private Secretary; they had four children (their granddaughter is the actress Helena Bonham Carter). Despite her heartbreak, Violet remained WSC's closest female friend and they saw each other regularly. She was active in the Liberal Party, rising to become its first female president from 1945 to 1947. She also stood for Parliament twice but lost in both 1945 and 1951 (even though, on the latter occasion, WSC persuaded the Conservative Party not to post anyone against her, she still lost to the Labour candidate).

✌ The Sister-in-Law

Lady Gwendoline Bertie (known as 'Goonie') was the daughter of the Earl of Abingdon, a Catholic nobleman. She had had a brief flirtation with WSC, but married his brother Jack in August 1908 (one month before WSC and Clemmie's wedding). 'Goonie' and Jack had three children; in 1952, their youngest, Clarissa, would become Anthony Eden's second wife.

THE BEST FRIEND

Frederick Edwin Smith (known as 'F.E.', and raised to the peerage as Baron Birkenhead in 1919) was a Conservative politician and a leading barrister, commanding huge fees (he represented WSC's mother Jennie in her divorce case with her second husband, George Cornwallis-West). After F.E. became an MP in 1906 he became friends with WSC, even though they were then on opposite sides of the aisle. F.E. lived just down the road from WSC, and they served in the same yeomanry cavalry regiment, the Queen's Own Oxfordshire Hussars. Clemmie was somewhat disapproving of F.E., believing his bad habits like heavy drinking and gambling rubbed off on WSC, but she could not doubt F.E.'s constant loyalty. F.E.'s premature death in 1930 at the age of fifty-eight, from pneumonia that arose from cirrhosis of the liver, robbed WSC of a faithful friend and advisor.

✌ Lord Beaverbrook

The newspaper publisher Max Aitken, Baron Beaverbrook, was one of the most influential figures in Britain during the first half of the twentieth century. Born in Canada, he made a fortune in cement and went on to own the *Daily Express*. He was introduced to WSC by F.E. in 1911 and they became close friends. Despite their political differences, particularly over appeasement, WSC had enough faith in Beaverbrook to appoint him Minister of Aircraft Production from 1940 to 1941 and Minister of Supply from 1941 to 1942.

THE PROF

Frederick Lindemann was the son of a German engineer who became a naturalized British subject. In 1919 he was appointed a professor of physics at Oxford and the director of the famed Clarendon Laboratory. A life-long bachelor, he was a skilled tennis player (once making it through to the second round of the men's doubles at Wimbledon). Lindemann was introduced to WSC in 1921 at a dinner held by their mutual acquaintance the Duke of Westminster. Lindemann became a regular weekend guest at Chartwell from 1932, although when he visited, the chef had to allow for his strict vegetarian diet and prepare dishes that primarily featured egg whites, skinned tomatoes, waxy potatoes and fresh mayonnaise. Lindemann was also teetotal, but would make an allowance for WSC and consume precisely 32 cubic centimetres of brandy after dining. As he would only sleep in his own bed, he would return to Oxford every night. Lindemann was also responsible for arranging Albert Einstein's 1933 lunch with WSC at Chartwell.

Lindemann's great value for WSC was his ability to boil down complex matters, even nuclear physics, into simple and understandable terms while retaining all essential information. When WSC became Prime Minister, Lindemann became a key advisor, met with him almost daily and regularly attended War Cabinet meetings. Lindemann established S-Branch, which trawled through thousands of reports to produce charts and statistics on almost every aspect of the war effort, from food supply to weapon production. Despite his undoubted intellect, Lindemann was difficult and abrasive, with few friends aside from WSC. His personal beliefs were also problematic: he was a proponent of eugenics and a racist. He also persuaded WSC to divert shipments from the Indian Ocean to the Atlantic to ensure Britain's food supply. This contributed to famine in Bengal and British colonies in East Africa, which killed millions.

✌ Gandhi

Mahatma Gandhi was the father of Indian independence, but WSC viewed him with disdain. They first met in 1906 when WSC was Secretary of State for the Colonies and Gandhi came to London to protest against the finger-printing of Indians in South Africa and other racist policies against them. WSC, not wishing to be drawn into dispute with the Boers, did little. He was a consistent opponent of Indian independence, believing British rule was beneficial and that Indians were not ready for self-government. When Gandhi visited England again in 1931, WSC refused to meet him. At this time WSC described Gandhi as a seditious, half-naked, fakir.

THE BODYGUARD

Walter Thompson grew up in Brixton, South London, and in 1913 joined the police's Special Branch. His activities included monitoring foreign subversives, counter-espionage and guarding visiting foreign dignitaries. In 1921 he was given his most challenging assignment: acting as WSC's personal bodyguard. Thompson spent the next eleven years at WSC's side, saving his life several times. The challenge of the job and its long hours placed a great strain on Thompson's health, and contributed to the break-up of his first marriage in 1929. He subsequently married Mary Shearburn, one of WSC's secretaries.

Thompson initially retired in 1935, and started a grocer's in Norwood, south London. In August 1939, just before the outbreak of war, WSC requested that Thompson come out of retirement to act as his bodyguard again. Thompson agreed, and was paid £5 per week and given WSC's own Colt automatic pistol (he was the only man WSC allowed to handle the guns in his personal armoury). When a state of emergency was declared soon after, Thompson rejoined the police, allowing him to use his preferred official sidearm, a Webley .32 revolver. Thompson remained at WSC's side for the rest of the war, successfully keeping him safe from harm.

WINSTON'S FAITHFUL DISCIPLE

One of the most colourful figures in WSC's entourage was Brendan Bracken, a lanky Irishman with flame-red hair. He kept his true origins shrouded in mystery, hinting that he might be WSC's illegitimate son (he was actually the son of a Tipperary stonemason). Bracken first met WSC in 1923 at a dinner hosted by the editor of *The Observer*. At the time, the twenty-two-year-old Bracken was working as a magazine editor, but he soon became WSC's fixer and factotum. Clemmie never liked Bracken, and he was not welcome at the Churchills' London home, although he was a constant presence at Chartwell. Bracken served as a Conservative MP from 1929 to 1952 and was Minister of Information from 1941 to 1945, playing a key role in Churchill's War Ministry, particularly in forging good relations with the USA. He combined this with a successful career in publishing; he was a founder editor of the magazine *The Banker* in 1926 and established the modern version of the *Financial Times* in 1945. Made a viscount in 1952, Bracken died of oesophageal cancer six years later, leaving much of his estate to Churchill College.

✌ The Terrible Bs

Along with Birkenhead and Beaverbrook, Brendan Bracken formed a trio called the 'Terrible Bs' – the term Clemmie used to refer to the group of WSC's friends of whom she most disapproved.

A HOST ON THE RIVIERA

Emery Reves (born in Hungary in 1904 as Révész Imre) was a writer and publisher introduced to WSC in 1937. He was a staunch opponent of fascism and a supporter of world federalism as a way to preserve international peace. His magazine

Cooperation had a strong anti-Nazi stance, and published many articles by WSC. Reves then became WSC's literary agent, negotiating lucrative payments for the foreign rights to his post-war books. Reves's Côte d'Azur villa, known as La Pausa (which he purchased from Coco Chanel in 1953), became one of WSC's favourite destinations. He visited ten times from 1956 to 1960, often staying for several weeks to write, paint and relax. Reves's long-term partner was Wendy Russell, an American model. Unfortunately, Clemmie developed a strong dislike of her, which contributed to the friendship between WSC and Emery cooling, and ended the holidays at La Pausa.

THE SAVIOUR OF CHARTWELL

B y 1938 WSC's finances were in dire straits. A recession in the USA reduced the value of shares he had purchased on the New York Stock Exchange from £18,000 to £6,000. He was forced to put his beloved Chartwell on the market for £20,000. At this point Bracken introduced WSC to Sir Henry Strakosch, a naturalized Austrian-born banker and financial journalist. Strakosch was a great admirer of WSC's anti-fascism and agreed to take over WSC's American holdings at their original purchase price while paying him £800 per year and giving him the option to re-purchase them if he wished. This saved WSC from having to sell Chartwell. When Strakosch died in 1943 he left WSC £20,000 (worth around £800,000 today).

✌ The Inside Man

While in political exile in the 1930s, WSC continued to be kept informed about foreign affairs through Desmond Morton, a high-level intelligence official whom he had met on the Western Front during the First World War. Morton's leaks gave WSC the in-depth knowledge he needed to speak out against appeasement.

A QUARRELSOME ALLY

Charles de Gaulle, the self-proclaimed saviour of France, frequently clashed with WSC. They first met on 9 June 1940 at 10 Downing Street when de Gaulle flew to London to coordinate a last-ditch defence against the German forces. Although WSC refused to release more British and Commonwealth troops or air squadrons, de Gaulle still came away from the meeting believing he had a firm and steadfast confederate. They met several more times that month and WSC allowed de Gaulle to use the BBC for his famed Appeal of 18 June, which urged France to resist the German occupation.

The war-time disputes between WSC and de Gaulle are too numerous to detail here. Key points of disagreement included the Royal Navy's pre-emptive attack on the French fleet at Mers-el-Kébir in Algeria, keeping details of D-Day obscure and de Gaulle's perceived dictatorial tendencies. Despite this, in 1958 de Gaulle bestowed on WSC the Cross of the Liberation, reopening the award especially for him as it had been closed since 1946. De Gaulle gifted WSC a glass Gallic cockerel, which became a treasured possession. Their last meeting was in September 1960, while WSC was in southern France. After WSC died, de Gaulle sent a handwritten note to Clemmie every year on the anniversary of his death.

TEDDY ROOSEVELT

While WSC was touring the United States in 1900, he was invited to dinner by Theodore Roosevelt, then Governor of New York. The man who would become President the next year immediately took against WSC, writing disparagingly of him in letters and refusing to meet him when he travelled to London as the representative of the American government at Edward VII's funeral.

✌ An Inauspicious Beginning to a Great Friendship

Franklin D. Roosevelt, then a thirty-six-year-old and Assistant Secretary of the US Navy, visited London in 1918. He met WSC, already a senior politician, at a banquet at Gray's Inn. His first impressions were not favourable; FDR recalled that he thought WSC was a 'stinker' with a lordly attitude. WSC claimed to not remember the meeting.

DR WILSON

WSC's health was never completely robust, and his travails as a war-time leader put it under huge strain. His personal physician from 1940 to 1965 was Sir Charles McMoran Wilson, one of the foremost doctors in the country. He travelled with WSC on most of his foreign trips, always bringing his golf clubs with him to entertain himself if his services were not needed. He did not accept payment, although he did receive compensation for travel. As a reward he was created Baron Moran in 1943 and WSC set up a covenant for his family. The year after WSC died, Moran published a detailed account of his health called *The Struggle for Survival*, which many believed was a breach of doctor–patient confidentiality.

BESSIE BRADDOCK

A Liverpudlian Labour MP, 'Battling Bessie' was an outspoken socialist, trade unionist and one of the best-known women in England. It is reported that in 1946 she accused WSC of being 'disgustingly drunk', to which he replied that at least he would be sober in the morning, while she would still be 'disgustingly ugly'. It is likely the exchange was apocryphal, as the joke had been doing the rounds since the 1880s.

In a similar incident in 1940, Nancy Astor, the first female MP to sit in Parliament (and later a supporter of fascism), is said to have told WSC that if they were married she would poison his coffee. WSC ostensibly replied that if he were her husband, he would drink it. Like the Braddock *bon mot*, this is simply the placing of an old joke (this one dating back to 1900) into the mouths of current celebrities.

✌ Elizabeth II

WSC met the future queen for the first time in September 1928 while at Balmoral shooting with her father George VI. He wrote to Clemmie that the girl, even though she was just two, already had an air of authority. A quarter of a century later, Elizabeth II honoured WSC by making him a Knight of the Garter. She also commissioned a bust of WSC, which was placed in her collection at Windsor Castle alongside those of Marlborough, Nelson and Wellington.

CHAPTER 3

Writer and Soldier

THE BRUCE SCANDAL

In 1895 a group of officers in the Fourth Hussars, supposedly led by WSC (who had joined the regiment that February), took out Allan Bruce, a potential new member of the regiment, for dinner at a London club. It was alleged they were trying to force Bruce to serve elsewhere, as they believed he was not suitable for the regiment because his allowance of £500 was too low (this was somewhat hypocritical on WSC's part, as his allowance was also £500). Bruce joined the regiment anyway, but was soon charged with misconduct and compelled to resign. His father, a barrister called A. C. Bruce-Pryce, stated that the real reason for his son's rejection was that he knew that WSC had been engaged in 'gross immorality of the Oscar Wilde type' while at Sandhurst. WSC sued for libel, and settled out of court for £500 and a letter of apology.

FIRST COMBAT

The Cuban War of Independence began in February 1895, and saw Spanish colonial forces fight against Cuban nationalists (supported by the USA). In November WSC travelled across the Atlantic with his fellow officer Reggie Barnes to observe the fighting. WSC's ticket cost £37; he persuaded his mother Jennie to give it to him as an early birthday present, saying that going to Cuba would be cheaper than a couple of months hunting in England, as well as safer. After arriving in New York, WSC and Barnes travelled to Key West and then took a ship to Havana, arriving there on 20 November. WSC spent his twenty-first birthday in Cuba, where he had his first taste of being under fire.

While in Havana, WSC and Barnes were given permission to join a Spanish contingent led by General Suárez Valdés, so travelled by train to meet them at Sancti Spíritus in central Cuba. Officially they were 'guests', so could only use their weapons in self-defence. WSC and Barnes joined Suárez Valdés and his men as they marched across the country, stopping at 9 a.m. for coffee and stew. Afterwards, the general's aide-de-camp produced a long metal bottle containing a rum cocktail (WSC's first taste of the drink). Everyone had a drink and then hammocks were slung up between trees and the entire party slept for four hours (WSC enthusiastically adopted siestas for the rest of his life, almost always sleeping for at least a short time during the day). While they were sleeping, rebels approached and attacked the slumbering group. Fortunately, WSC and the Spanish all survived the ambush.

WSC and the Spanish were shot at again a few days later while bathing on 1 December, and the next day WSC witnessed a full-scale engagement, at the Battle of La Reforma. When the fighting started WSC and Barnes stuck close to Suárez Valdés, who daringly exposed himself to enemy fire. Both men were awarded a medal for gallantry called the Red Cross by the Spanish, although they were not permitted to wear it with their British Army uniforms.

WSC and Barnes spent seven weeks in Cuba before returning to England to join their regiment in the new year.

✌ To Print!

WSC's time in Cuba provided material for his first journalistic publication, which appeared on 13 December 1895 in the *Daily Graphic*. For this and the four subsequent reports in the newspaper, he was paid 25 guineas (equivalent to around £3,000).

LIFE IN INDIA

In October 1896 WSC arrived at Bangalore in southern India, the new base for the Fourth Hussars. He would leave Bangalore (and indeed India) for the final time in March 1899. While stationed in India, he managed two periods of home leave, an expedition to the North-West Frontier Province, three winter visits to Kolkata and a trip to Hyderabad to play polo.

WSC was largely bored and unhappy in Bangalore. His regiment saw no military action, and his official duties were undemanding, taking only three hours per day and usually complete by 10.30 a.m. WSC made little effort to engage with Indian culture or learn the language, and seldom left the cantonment where he shared a bungalow with Reggie Barnes. His main priority appears to have been polo, a game which he loved and excelled at. He also spent a great deal of time reading, digesting political news from home and ploughing through histories by Macaulay and Gibbon as well as works by Plato, Aristotle, Darwin, Adam Smith, Schopenhauer and Malthus. Other ways he passed the time included rose-gardening and collecting butterflies (he gathered sixty-five different species).

WSC grumbled about the state of the officers' mess, stating it needed a new carpet, cleaner tablecloths and better-quality cigarettes. His indolence and complaints irritated many of his fellow officers, and culminated in an incident where some attempted to squash WSC under a sofa in the mess (he escaped). WSC managed to make some amends by arranging a concert to raise money for the regimental fund. He opened the evening with a rendition of 'Oh, Listen to the Band' that he performed wearing morning dress with a carnation in his buttonhole.

✌ Prodigious Verbosity

WSC had a vocabulary of over 65,000 words. When President John F. Kennedy made him an honorary citizen of the USA in 1963 he paid tribute to WSC's skill as a wordsmith, saying 'he mobilized the English language and sent it into battle'.

THE MALAKAND FIELD FORCE

The North-West Frontier Province, on the border between British India and Afghanistan, was peopled by fiercely independent Pashtun tribes that regularly rebelled against the local British forces. In July 1897 they attacked the British garrison stationed in the region of Malakand. The experienced soldier Sir Bindon Blood (who had served in every British campaign since the 1870s) was charged with leading a field force to stamp out the uprising. At the time, WSC was home in London on leave, but he was keen for combat experience. His mother arranged for him to join the field force, although Blood insisted that the inexperienced young officer be attached as a journalist rather than a soldier.

WSC spent six weeks with the field force, filing fifteen dispatches for the *Daily Telegraph* (for which he was paid £5 apiece). He came under fire ten times, and was mentioned in dispatches for bravery. The articles he wrote were compiled into WSC's first book, *The Story of the Malakand Field Force*, published in 1898. His first advance (negotiated by his mother) was just £50.

✌ The Other Winston Churchill

In 1871 a baby was born in St Louis, Missouri, and named Winston Churchill. As an adult, and after serving in the US Navy, he became a popular novelist during the 1890s. When the coincidence was brought to their attention, the two Churchills began to correspond. From spring 1899, to avoid confusion, WSC began to publish under the name 'Winston Spencer Churchill', eventually shortened to 'Winston S. Churchill'. The American and British Churchills met in person in Boston in 1900. WSC told the American that he planned to be Prime Minister, and that he should try to be US President at the same time. The American Winston Churchill did indeed embark on a political career but it was largely unsuccessful; his highest elected office was in the New Hampshire state legislature.

TO THE SUDAN

The Sudanese Mahdists were followers of the Muslim religious leader Muhammad Ahmad, who had proclaimed himself to be the 'Mahdi', a messianic figure who would redeem Islam. They fought for the independence of Sudan, which was claimed by Egypt. Britain was drawn into the conflict after their 1882 occupation of Egypt. After years of sporadic fighting, in March 1898 an Anglo-Egyptian army set out to defeat the Mahdists and establish colonial dominion over Sudan. Its leader was Herbert Kitchener, who had been serving in the Middle East since the 1870s.

As Britain had not fought a major war in over a decade, soldiers all across the Empire wanted to join in the expedition. WSC was no different; however, as well as winning glory in combat he also wanted to write about it. From India, he requested a transfer to a regiment bound for Sudan, the 21st Lancers. This was approved by the War Office but rejected by Kitchener. WSC took leave to return to Britain to lobby for the transfer, arriving in London in June. Friends and family (including his mother) spoke up for WSC, and even Prime Minister Salisbury supported his cause. Kitchener, the son of an Irish army officer, still refused to accept him, possibly because he resented the young aristocrat's entitlement and social connections (he also loathed all journalists). Ultimately, WSC forced his way into the 21st Lancers when Sir Evelyn Wood, a high-ranking general in England who had authority over appointments to the regiment, named him as the replacement for an officer who died in Sudan in July. WSC was with his new regiment by August. Before he left, he had arranged to write reports for the *Morning Post*. This would finance the trip, as the War Office would not pay his expenses (as well as declining any liability if WSC was wounded or killed).

On 2 September WSC took part in the decisive engagement of the war, the Battle of Omdurman. Although outnumbered two-to-one, Kitchener's forces were armed with modern artillery, rifles and machine guns. When the Mahdists advanced, these new weapons cut through their lines, killing thousands. When they retreated, Kitchener sent the 21st Lancers, including WSC, in pursuit. After the battle, wounded Mahdists were left to die or shot or bayoneted where they lay. These actions were approved by Kitchener; WSC was shocked at his callousness, and criticized him in print. WSC returned to London in October to complete his leave before travelling back to India that December. Shortly afterwards the British Army instituted a regulation forbidding serving officers from simultaneously working as war correspondents. This contributed to WSC's decision to resign his commission so that he could pursue writing (as well as politics).

✌ *The River War*

As his time in the Army was coming to an end, WSC had been researching a book that would detail his time in Sudan as well as the history of Britain's recent activities there. He left India in March 1899 and arrived in England the next month. On the way home he had spent two weeks in Egypt where he spent time with Lord Cromer, the British Consul-General, who provided comments and suggestions on the text. *The River War* was published in two volumes in November 1899. The critical reaction was generally positive, although one review called WSC's writing 'ponderous and pretentious'.

SAVROLA

WSC only made one attempt at fiction, a novel called *Savrola*, which he began to write on the voyage from Britain to India in August 1897. After he finished it, the novel was serialized in the literary periodical *Macmillan's Magazine* and published as a book in February 1900. *Savrola* was a political adventure-romance set in a fictional Mediterranean republic called Laurania. The eponymous hero was a writer and politician who aimed to launch a democratic uprising against a dictator called General Antonio Molara.

In the midst of the intrigue, Savrola fell in love with Molara's wife, Lucile. Eventually a rebel army invaded, leading to civil war. Involved in the uprising was a secret socialist society headed by a radical anarchist called Karl Kreutze, who was responsible for the assassination of Molara. The country then descended into turmoil; the Lauranian Navy, loyal to Molara, threatened to bombard the capital unless Savrola was arrested and handed over. Fortunately for him, Savrola escaped and fled the country with Lucile, leading to the Navy shelling the capital. The story then ends somewhat abruptly, with a brief postscript explaining that peace was restored and Savrola eventually welcomed home.

Savrola initially earned WSC an advance of £250 and a further £100 for serialization. Despite the novel's lack of literary merit and WSC's dwindling enthusiasm for it (he urged friends not to read it), in 1908 his fame as a politician led to an illustrated paperback edition that earned him a further £225. Although WSC was usually eager to earn income from his writing, in 1940 he discouraged another reprint. *Savrola* was later adapted for television in the USA in 1956 and the BBC produced a radio drama in 1964.

SOUTH AFRICA

In October 1899 war erupted in South Africa between Britain and the independent Boer Republics of Orange Free State and Transvaal. WSC, out of the Army and fresh from being defeated in the 1899 Oldham by-election, covered the conflict for the *Morning Post* (he was paid £250 per month for his work). After sailing to Cape Town he travelled inland to report from Ladysmith, where a British garrison was being besieged by the Boers. On 15 November, while travelling around the region, his train was ambushed and derailed by the Boers. WSC was captured and held at a POW camp in the grounds of a teacher-training college in Pretoria. On 12 December he scaled the walls and escaped Pretoria by stowing away on a freight train. A starving WSC disembarked at the mining town of Witbank to look for food. By this time he was wanted dead or alive and there was a £25 bounty on his head. Fortunately for him, he came across the home of John Howard, an English mine manager, who agreed to feed and shelter him. WSC was hidden first down a mine, then in an office (where he found time to read the novel *Kidnapped* by Robert Louis Stevenson). After six days he was placed aboard a train (hidden in a consignment of wool) bound for Portuguese East Africa (modern Mozambique), where he arrived on 21 December.

WSC then sailed to Durban and joined the South African Light Horse regiment as a lieutenant, serving alongside his brother Jack and cousin Sunny. That February WSC took part in the Relief of Ladysmith before joining in the capture of Pretoria in June. After Pretoria fell, the war had transitioned to a bitter guerrilla conflict between Boer commandos and British and Commonwealth forces.

To defeat the Boer the British commander, Lord Kitchener, resorted to harsh and inhumane scorched earth tactics. Boer farms were burned and civilians were placed into concentration camps. The Second Boer War, which most in Britain had believed would be a short conflict, finally finished in May 1902.

Meanwhile, as the war raged on, WSC had left South Africa and on 20 July 1900 he arrived back in Britain, where as a result of his escape he had become a national celebrity. He spent the summer engaging in his successful campaign to be elected MP for Oldham. While still in South Africa, an account of his capture and escape had been published as *London to Ladysmith via Pretoria* that May. It was followed in October by *Ian Hamilton's March*, which further detailed his experiences in South Africa.

✌ Winston the Playwright?

In March 1900 WSC mentioned in a letter to Pamela Plowden that he planned to write a play set in South Africa, with the Second Boer War as a backdrop. He wanted it to be produced by the famed theatre manager Herbert Beerbohm Tree (who went on to found RADA and whose grandson was the actor Oliver Reed) and to feature realistic sets. However, Jennie Churchill convinced her son that the play would be seen as in poor taste, and he abandoned the project.

WINSTON ON TOUR

After he was first elected as an MP in October 1900, WSC, rather than rushing to take his seat, embarked on a lecture tour. In the first leg he criss-crossed the United Kingdom, travelling as far north as Dundee (eight years later he would be its MP), as far south as Plymouth and across the Irish Sea to Belfast and Dublin. He used a magic lantern (an early type of projector) to illustrate his South African adventures, and usually earned £100 for each night's performance (although he managed to pull in triple that for his performance at the Philharmonic Hall in Liverpool).

In December he took his talents to North America. His tour's itinerary took in Boston, Hartford, Fall River, New Bedford, Montreal, Ottawa, Toronto, Ann Arbor, Chicago, Milwaukee, Minneapolis, Winnipeg, St Louis, Baltimore, Washington DC, Philadelphia and New York. Some stops were more successful than others; in Hartford his share of the box office was just £10, while in Winnipeg (where he heard of the illness and death of Queen Victoria in January 1901) he sold 1,000 tickets – a staggering number given that the city's population was just 50,000.

WSC's promoter was Major James Pond, who had won the Medal of Honor during the American Civil War. Pond had previously managed speaking tours for such luminaries as Mark Twain, Dr Henry Morton Stanley and Arthur Conan Doyle. Pond and WSC had frequent arguments over money, which led to WSC cancelling a sold-out show in Brantford, Ontario. Pond was also irritated that WSC drank a pint of champagne with breakfast every morning. Despite these wrangles, when WSC returned home in February he was £10,000 richer.

☙ An Early Biography

The first of many biographies of WSC was published in 1905 when he was a thirty-year-old junior minister in the Colonial Office. The author, Alexander MacCallum Scott, marked out his subject as a future Prime Minister.

ANCESTRAL BIOGRAPHIES

In 1903 WSC was paid an advance of £8,000 to write a biography of his father Lord Randolph Churchill. The lucrative deal had been handled by Frank Harris, an Irish author and editor with an exuberant handlebar moustache who was an old associate of Lord Randolph's. He had recently suffered losses trying to open a hotel in Monaco, which made the deal particularly important for him. WSC paid him a commission of £400 for his part in the negotiations.

WSC's social status gave him access to official papers unavailable to the public. Many of his father's contemporaries were still alive and assisted by providing access to documents and letters as well as permission for WSC to use them; Salisbury, Edward VII and Joseph Chamberlain were all particularly helpful. When *Lord Randolph Churchill* was published, in two volumes, in 1906, it garnered mostly favourable reviews. However, Teddy Roosevelt, who had taken against WSC since meeting him in 1900, described both the subject and the book as 'cheap and vulgar'.

THE MARLBOROUGH SERIES

WSC's other great biographical project was about his ancestor John Churchill, the first Duke of Marlborough. It was begun in 1929 but work on the project did not start in earnest until 1932. That summer WSC travelled to Central Europe to tour the battlefields where Marlborough had made his name. On the trip, while staying at Munich, he witnessed a Nazi Party procession and nearly met his future nemesis Adolf Hitler, who was already a major figure in Germany and would become Chancellor the next year. WSC's son Randolph, who had joined his father, was acquainted with Hitler's foreign press secretary Ernst Hanfstaengl. Hanfstaengl met the Churchills for dinner at their hotel; he had asked Hitler to join them as well but Hitler decided not to attend.

The first of four volumes of *Marlborough: His Life and Times* was published in 1933 (the others followed in 1934, 1936 and 1938). It was published in Britain by Harrap, who paid WSC a £10,000 advance. Scribner's paid WSC an advance of £5,000 for the American rights. These were staggering amounts (worth a combined total of over £750,000 today), and both firms appear to have somewhat over-estimated public interest in the great duke. By 1939 there were still hundreds of copies left unsold and in the USA even two decades later the book had not sold enough to earn back the advance.

MY EARLY LIFE

In between the publication of these two biographies WSC wrote a work of autobiography. *My Early Life* (known as *A Roving Commission* in the USA) covered the period from his birth in 1874 to his first years as an MP in 1902. It formed the basis of Richard Attenborough's 1972 feature film *Young Winston*.

THE WORLD CRISIS

To negotiate the deal for his multi-volume history of the First World War, titled *The World Crisis* and published from 1923 to 1931, WSC used the literary agent Curtis Brown. He wanted at least £20,000, but between them they procured an even higher sum: an advance of £9,000 for the British edition from Thornton Butterworth, £8,000 from Scribner's for the American edition, and £13,000 for serialization rights on both sides of the Atlantic. In total this gave him £27,000. *The World Crisis* was also released in translation in French, German, Italian, Russian, Danish, Czech, Finnish, Norwegian, Swedish and Spanish. The initial payments for the project gave WSC the funds to purchase Chartwell in 1922, as well as a new Rolls-Royce.

WRITING AT CHARTWELL

WSC made Chartwell his literary HQ. The nerve-centre was his study on the top floor overlooking the gardens and grounds. It was 30 feet by 15 feet, with 20-foot-high ceilings, lined with book shelves and decorated with busts of Napoleon and Nelson. Close by was a telephone exchange, offices for a team of six researchers and a 60,000-volume library. WSC tended to do most of his initial composition via dictation to his secretaries after dinner and drinks, starting at 10 p.m. and working until about 2 a.m. During the day he would edit the typewritten manuscript by hand, usually working in bed in the morning, before sending it to the publisher. They would return WSC a typescript, which he would give a final edit to at his standing desk.

✌ Money for Nothing

From 1932 to 1933 WSC was commissioned by the *News of the World* to condense several classic novels in a series called 'Great Stories of the World Retold' at a rate of £333 per article. However, his former private secretary Edward Marsh did all the writing for him, receiving just £25 apiece. The articles were later syndicated in the *Chicago Tribune*, netting WSC another £1,800.

THE IMPORTANCE OF PRECISION

WSC was exacting about linguistic style and usage. As Prime Minister he ensured that the 'Local Defence Volunteers' became known as the more evocative 'Home Guard'. Thanks to WSC, war-time workers' canteens were called 'British Restaurants' instead of 'Communal Feeding Centres' (which he thought sounded too socialist). Even during the preparations for D-Day he found time to correct an official document that had used the word 'intensive' when 'intense' was the correct word. His linguistic bible was Henry Watson Fowler's influential style guide *A Dictionary of Modern English Usage* – he even gave a copy to the future Elizabeth II as her Christmas present in 1940.

THE SECOND WORLD WAR

From 1948 to 1953 WSC's six-volume history of the Second World War was published. He and his team of assistants were allowed access to official documents on condition that no sensitive state secrets be revealed and that the copy could be vetted before publication. It was highly anticipated; the first volume, *The Gathering Storm*, sold 530,000 hardback copies when it appeared in June 1948. The lucrative publication and serialization deals for the work were negotiated by his friend and literary agent Emery Reves. Its huge sales delivered WSC from the financial worries that had previously occasionally arisen as a result of his expensive lifestyle and failed investments.

Much of the writing activity for this project took place abroad, on trips paid for by his American publishers. The first ran from 10

December 1947 to 19 January 1948, when WSC flew to Morocco with his daughter Sarah, his literary assistant William Deakin and two secretaries (Jo Sturdee and Elizabeth Gilliatt). They stayed at one of WSC's favourite places, the Hotel Mamounia in Marrakesh. To pay for his expenses, *Life*, who held the American serialization rights, opened a local bank account in his name (at the time there were restrictions on spending the Pound Sterling abroad); in total WSC drew $13,600 from it (this did not include funding his private aeroplane, which was paid for by an admirer, the Australian mining tycoon William Sydney Robinson). Over the next few years, WSC took several other similar writing trips, to destinations such as Aix-en-Provence, Lake Garda, Monte Carlo, the French Alps and Venice.

✌ An Encouraging Acronym

One of WSC's favourite exhortations to his staff in challenging moments was to 'keep buggering on', which he shortened to 'KBO'.

THE NOBEL PRIZE

After publication of his history of the Second World War was completed, WSC was awarded the Nobel Prize for Literature. This was slightly unusual because at the time WSC was the sitting Prime Minister, and individuals who held high political office were customarily not considered. However, by this time WSC had been in the running several times, so on 15 October 1953 the Swedish Academy made the decision to give him the prize. WSC was eager to visit Stockholm (one of the few European capitals he had not been to) that December to accept the prize in person and attend the celebratory banquet hosted by King Gustaf V, but was ultimately unable to travel to Sweden because he had to attend the 1953 Bermuda Conference to meet with the American and French presidents. Clemmie and their youngest daughter, Mary, travelled to accept the award on WSC's behalf. At the banquet Clemmie read out a speech written by WSC that was greeted by waves of applause.

A CHALLENGING PROJECT

Perhaps WSC's most ambitious literary enterprise was *A History of the English-Speaking Peoples*. In just four volumes it told the story of Britain and its colonies (including former ones such as the USA) from Julius Caesar's invasion in 55 BCE to the start of the First World War. He began the project in 1937 but his work was delayed by the outbreak of the Second World War. WSC even sold the movie rights to the director Sir Alexander Korda for £50,000 in 1944; however, a feature film never materialized. The four volumes were eventually published between 1956 and 1958; all were bestsellers.

A PRODIGIOUS OUTPUT

In total, WSC wrote fifty-eight books. His oeuvre comprised:

Seven memoirs
Sixteen historical volumes
Twenty-two volumes of his speeches
Four collections of newspaper and magazine articles
Two volumes of essays
Six volumes of biography
One novel

WSC also wrote 842 articles, about one-quarter of which were reports of warfare in Cuba, India, Sudan and South Africa. In total, he wrote more than Charles Dickens and William Shakespeare combined.

CHAPTER 4

Churchillian Recreation

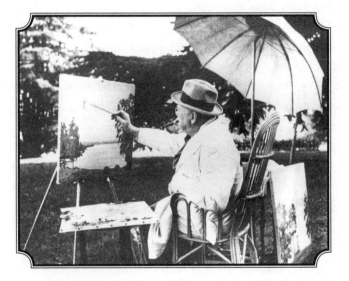

THE THESPIAN

When WSC was thirteen his mother's sisters, Leonie and Clara, gave him a toy stage. He used it to give performances to friends and family for another four years. A love of the stage ran in the family; WSC's mother grew up with a 600-seat private theatre in her family's New York mansion and wrote a play called *His Borrowed Plumes*, which opened in London in 1909 (it was a commercial failure).

Thirty-six years later, WSC received two standing ovations in a London theatre. However, these were as an audience member while attending a production of Noël Coward's *Private Lives*, shortly after being defeated in the 1945 General Election.

✌ A Forceful Player

While a student at Harrow, WSC was fond of playing billiards, but he hit the ball so hard that it would often shoot off the table and shatter windows. He also enjoyed a tabletop game called Corinthian bagatelle, which involved trying to fire small metal balls past pins into holes.

WAR GAMES

One of WSC's greatest foes, evident from his early years, was his own accident-proneness. In the winter of 1892–3, he was staying at Canford Manor in Dorset, the home of his maternal aunt Lady Cornelia, who had married the Welsh industrialist Ivor Guest, Baron Wimborne. WSC, who was eighteen at the time (and frankly old enough to know better), was playing a game of chase with his brother Jack and a cousin. He was cornered on a bridge and tried to escape by vaulting over a railing and jumping for a pine tree, hoping to slide down to safety. He missed and fell thirty feet, rupturing a kidney. He spent three days in a coma before recovering.

SWISS HIKES

In August 1893, while waiting to hear if he had got into Sandhurst at his third attempt, WSC went on a hiking holiday through Switzerland and Northern Italy with his brother Jack and a young language tutor from Eton called J. D. G. Little. In Lucerne WSC found out that he had passed. Notes and telegrams of congratulation flooded in from friends and family. However, Lord Randolph, who was staying at a resort at the Bavarian spa town of Bad Kissingen, was, as mentioned earlier, irritated that his son had not achieved enough marks to train to become an infantry officer, but instead would enter the cavalry. When WSC reached Milan he received a vituperative letter from his father upbraiding him for his perceived failure and chastising him for his poor academic performance.

Despite his father's reaction, the holiday could have been a whole lot worse. One day, WSC rowed out on Lake Geneva with a friend, and after travelling a mile they jumped into the water for a swim. While they were paddling, the wind blew their boat away. WSC managed to catch up to it, clamber aboard and row back to fetch his companion, but it had been a close run thing – had the boat been blown further away, he could have drowned.

WSC returned to Switzerland several times to hike and enjoy the alpine scenery. A favourite destination was the Villa Cassel at Riederfurka. Built between 1900 and 1902, it was owned by Sir Ernest Cassel, a merchant banker born in Cologne who had become a naturalized British citizen. Cassel was one of the richest men in Europe, and a close friend and advisor of WSC's. His remote Swiss castle was the perfect retreat. Inaccessible by road, its luxurious fittings had to be carried by donkeys and porters over miles of alpine paths. In 1904 WSC spent a month at Cassel's villa, working on his biography of Lord Randolph in the mornings, before spending the rest of the day hiking, reading and playing bridge. WSC returned to Villa Cassel in 1906 and 1910. His next trip to Switzerland was in 1946, when he made his great speech at Zürich calling for the creation of a united Europe.

A SCANDALOUS STEEPLECHASE

WSC was an accomplished rider. As a junior officer he took part in the Fourth Hussars Subalterns' Challenge Cup, a steeplechase organized by the National Hunt Committee. Due to the large obstacles, steeplechases were dangerous affairs and WSC had promised his mother he would not take part in any. However, he could not resist the chance to take part in his first competitive race. Riding under the pseudonym 'Mr Spencer', WSC finished third. Shortly afterwards there was a minor scandal. The winning horse, a six-to-one outsider called Surefoot, was said to have not actually run the race! It was rumoured that he was swapped for a superior ringer at the last minute, allegedly so the participants in the ploy could make money betting on the result. The race was declared void and all the horses that participated were forbidden from taking part in future National Hunt events. Although WSC was probably not personally involved in the fraud, his proximity to the event would have done his reputation no favours.

THE EQUESTRIAN

Polo was WSC's real love, and he played a great deal of it in India. In 1898 his regiment won the Inter-Regimental Polo Tournament there. The other three riders on WSC's team were his friend Reggie Barnes (who rose to the rank of Major-General and served in the Army until 1921), Albert Savory (killed in action during the Second Boer War) and Reginald Hoare (who later commanded the Fourth Hussars from 1905 to 1909). WSC's success was all the more striking because on his first day in India he had seriously dislocated his shoulder when his landing craft had moved suddenly as he was climbing a ladder ashore. This meant he had to play polo with his upper arm strapped to his shoulder (later on, while giving a speech in the Commons, WSC nearly dislocated the shoulder again when making an expansive gesture). He carried on playing polo until he was fifty-two, taking part in his last game in January 1927 while in Malta on holiday.

✌ Cards

WSC's favourite card-game was bezique. Usually played by two players, bezique uses sixty-four cards (made up by combining two decks after removing the twos, threes, fours, fives and sixes from each). Players win by scoring points for various combinations of cards. WSC enjoyed a more complex version of bezique that used a deck made up of six packs. He also frequently played other card games; when visiting the USA in 1946 he played several hands of poker with Harry S. Truman on the presidential train.

WAGERS

L ike his father and most of his contemporaries, WSC was a keen gambler. Fortunately, the habit was never debilitating, and his debts were never excessive. One of WSC's most successful winning streaks was in Deauville in Normandy. He had travelled there in August 1906 as a guest of his friend Maurice, Baron de Forest, a noted figure of the time. Forest was born in France, the orphaned son of an American circus performer; he had been adopted by a wealthy banking family who resided in the Austro-Hungarian Empire. Forest was educated at Eton and Oxford and in 1900 was naturalized as a British citizen. Fabulously wealthy as a result of his inheritance, Forest was a keen motor-car driver and aviator as well as being a Liberal MP from 1911 to 1918. He became friends with WSC, who often stayed on his yacht and also visited his family residence near Brno (in the modern-day Czech Republic), including on his honeymoon with Clemmie. While in Deauville with Forest, WSC gambled at the Grand Casino until 5 a.m. every night for a week, gaining a profit of £260 (over £25,000 today).

WSC did not always play for high stakes; in 1941 while travelling to Newfoundland on the HMS *Prince of Wales* to meet FDR he lost £7 playing backgammon against the American diplomat Harry Hopkins.

✌ Golfing

In 1910 WSC (with the encouragement of David Lloyd George, who was a member) joined the Walton Golf Club in Surrey. He was never a keen player, although his handicap was a fairly respectable eighteen, and joined the club mainly to take part in the gossip and debate with other members (who included the likes of Arthur Balfour and Andrew Bonar Law, leading Conservatives who both served as Prime Minister – respectively, from 1902 to 1905 and 1922 to 1923), often staying in the clubhouse to rehearse speeches while his friends played.

THE RESERVIST

Yeomanry regiments are reserve volunteer cavalry forces, many of which date back to the later eighteenth century. In January 1902 WSC joined one of them, the Queen's Own Oxfordshire Hussars (QOOH), as a captain. The regiment's annual camp (held at Blenheim Palace) lasted one week. As well as keeping WSC and the rest of his fellow-volunteers fighting-fit, such occasions gave him a chance to drink and gamble with the other officers, who included his brother Jack, cousin Sunny and close friend F.E. Smith. In 1905 WSC became a major in the regiment, and until 1913 he commanded its Henley-on-Thames squadron. He served as a reserve officer until 1924, when he resigned from the Territorial Army.

WSC always paid close attention to the QOOH. Shortly after the First World War started, he intervened to ensure the regiment would be sent to serve on the Western Front. The regular army initially did not hold them in high regard, nicknaming the QOOH the 'Queer Objects On Horseback' or 'Agricultural Cavalry'. In 1922 the QOOH were converted from a cavalry into an artillery force. For much of the Second World War they served in England and Northern Ireland, until in October 1944 WSC personally requested they be sent to fight in France. WSC was the regiment's honorary colonel until his death and left instructions that they be given a place of distinction in the procession at his state funeral, immediately in front of his coffin.

✌ Beach-life

Aside from swimming, one of WSC's favourite pastimes at the beach was to dig in the sand. He would create sea battles or dam pretend rivers. In April 1911, while he was Home Secretary, WSC was visiting a beach in Anglesey and became immersed in his work digging up the sand. He was completely unaware that a large crowd had gathered to watch him, some even using opera glasses.

THE OTHER CLUB

In 1764 a dining club was established in London; its nine original members included the philosopher Edmund Burke, the lexicographer Dr Samuel Johnson and the artist Joshua Reynolds. Membership of the institution, known simply as 'The Club', could only be gained by unanimous election by members.

WSC and his friend F. E. Smith were thought too contentious for membership of The Club, so in 1911 they founded their own dining society, which they named 'The Other Club'. Charter members included Lloyd George, Kitchener and Sunny. Seeking to establish a bipartisan atmosphere, members were drawn from both the Liberals and Conservatives, and non-politicians were also invited. WSC and F.E. decided that membership should be based on conversational skill and sociability. The Other Club met at the Savoy Hotel on alternate Thursdays while Parliament was in session, but at times of political turmoil it gathered less frequently. After F.E. died in 1930, WSC largely decided on membership by himself. He even granted his friend Aristotle Onassis membership; Onassis only came to two meetings, although he did gift the club a great deal of champagne. WSC last attended The Other Club on 10 December 1964, just a few weeks before he died.

Whereas The Club has not met since the 1960s, The Other Club continues to gather to this day. Members have included politicians from across the political spectrum such as Paddy Ashdown, Tony Blair, Gordon Brown, Ken Clarke, Ted Heath, Chris Patten and John Smith as well as people from outside of Parliament such as the writer Max Hastings, the playwright Tom Stoppard and Charles, Prince of Wales.

THE AVIATOR

WSC was always interested in new technology, none more so than the aeroplane. While he was First Lord of the Admiralty, he was a great proponent of the adoption of aircraft for sea warfare and encouraged the Royal Navy to research and invest in airpower. His personal interest in aviation went even further; by 1913, despite the warnings of friends and family, he had started to take flying lessons, often going up several times a day. He was taking a huge risk; the aeroplane had been invented only a decade earlier, so engine failures, accidents and deaths were incredibly common. One of WSC's first instructors, Captain Gilbert Wildman-Lushington, who gave him lessons to raise money for his upcoming wedding, died in a crash on 30 November. The accident occurred just three days after a lesson with WSC. When the famed aviator Gustav Hamel (the son of Edward VII's physician) disappeared over the Channel in May 1914 while flying back to England from France, WSC ceased his lessons. However, it proved to be a hiatus rather than a permanent end to his dalliance with aviation.

In 1919 WSC resumed his flying lessons, hoping to win his pilot's licence. His instructor was the New Zealand-born Colonel Jack Scott, an ace during the First World War who had been awarded the Military Cross. On 18 July they took off from Croydon Aerodrome in an Airco DH.4, a two-seater aircraft with dual controls. Initially WSC was piloting, but shortly after take-off the aeroplane began to lose speed and fall rapidly. Scott took over control. Despite his efforts the aeroplane continued to plummet and crashed into the runway at fifty miles per hour. There was no explosion because the quick-thinking Scott had turned off the engine just before impact.

WSC was slammed forwards, but his safety-belt prevented death or severe injury; he was only seriously bruised. This time he gave up flying lessons for good.

THE PAINTER

When WSC was removed as First Lord of the Admiralty in May 1915 due to the failure of the Gallipoli Campaign, he found solace in a new hobby: painting. At the time, WSC was renting a country house called Hoe Farm, near Godalming in Surrey, where he spent weekends. On the suggestion of his sister-in-law Goonie, he took up painting that July. When he first approached the canvas he was nervous and reluctant to start. A visitor, the painter Hazel Lavery (wife of the famed Irish portrait artist Sir John Lavery), seeing WSC hesitating, picked up his brushes and began applying paint onto the canvas. From this point on, he lost all trepidation when it came to painting. An easel, canvas, paints and brushes accompanied him whenever he travelled. The activity took all of WSC's attention; his friend Violet Asquith said it was the only thing he would do in complete silence. He even wrote a short book about his hobby, *Painting as a Pastime*, which was a compilation of articles he had written on the subject for *Strand Magazine* from 1921 to 1922.

WSC produced around five hundred canvases in total; about half were painted in the 1930s. Oils were his preferred medium; he used them because it was easier to correct mistakes, as you could just scrape them off, and he liked being able to build layer upon layer of colour. His early works were of the countryside around Hoe Farm, and for the most part he concentrated on landscapes. However, he also painted portraits (his first was of John Lavery, which was WSC's earliest exhibited work, appearing in a 1919 Royal Society of Portrait Painters exhibition), still-life flowers and interiors (especially of Blenheim).

There was little time for painting during the Second World War; WSC completed just one picture as war-time leader. After the Casablanca Conference (14–24 January 1943) he persuaded FDR that they should travel together to see Marrakesh and the Atlas Mountains. They drove four hours south, stopping for a roadside picnic where they were guarded by armoured cars, soldiers with Tommy guns and patrolling aircraft. They stayed with the American Vice-Consul, whose residence had a tower that FDR was carried up so he could watch the sun set over the Atlas Mountains with WSC. The American President left the next day, while WSC returned to the tower to paint the scene they had enjoyed together. He later gifted the work, which he titled *A view of Marrakech, with the tower of the Katoubia mosque, January 1943*, to FDR.

✌ Artistic Honours

WSC certainly had talent. He won first prize at an amateur art competition in 1925 for a landscape of Chartwell entitled *Winter Sunshine*; there is no chance he won simply because of his name, as a condition of entry to the exhibition was that all works would be anonymous. In 1948 the Royal Academy made him an Honorary Academician Extraordinary and in 1959 he had a one-man show there. There is one of WSC's works in the Tate

Gallery's collection in London; a landscape called *The Loup River, Alpes Maritimes*.

BATHTIME

Hot baths were an essential part of WSC's routine. He insisted on at least one a day wherever he was, even at times of war. When he served on the Western Front in 1916 he brought with him his own bathtub, which was shaped like a long soap dish (he did allow others to use it, and it was frequently borrowed), as well as large towels and a hot-water bottle. During the Second World War, while visiting Egypt, WSC used the hot water from the boiler of a locomotive to bathe in. While visiting Bristol to survey the damage done by German bombing raids, he arrived at his hotel very early in the morning and requested a bath. The staff had to carry hot water up from the kitchen in pails, cans and jugs to fill the bath in his room. On long flights WSC would sometimes use a portable canvas bathtub.

Helpfully (for him at least), given his frequent baths, WSC had no qualms about walking from his bath to his rooms nude. At Chartwell in particular his staff were used to the sight of their boss striding around naked. WSC was just as uninhibited on his travels, which occasionally shocked his hosts. While staying at the White House in December 1941 WSC, fresh from his bath, was busily dictating a speech in the nude. At this moment President Roosevelt was wheeled into the room – seeing his guest naked he apologized and began to exit; WSC is said to have reassured the American President by saying it was now clear he had nothing to hide from him.

AN INTEREST IN SCIENCE FICTION

One of WSC's favourite writers H. G. Wells was an early progenitor of sci-fi. WSC said he had read all of Wells's books twice, and that *The Time Machine* was one he would take with him to Purgatory. WSC and Wells had met in 1900 and become friends. They fell out because of WSC's role in the Gallipoli Campaign and Wells's support for the Russian Revolution. In Wells's 1923 novel *Men Like Gods* there is a reckless and reactionary character called Rupert Catskill said to be modelled on WSC.

✌ ... and Real Science

In spring 1926 Frederick Lindemann sent WSC, then Chancellor of the Exchequer, a book about quantum theory and the structure of atoms. He was so consumed by it that he could not concentrate on the Budget he was supposed to be preparing.

BRICKLAYING

WSC found bricklaying soothing and relaxing. He had learned how to do it in the 1920s while building work was being done at Chartwell. He was taught by two of his employees (Messrs Kurn and Whitbread) and a professional bricklayer called Benny Barnes. He put the lessons to good use, personally laying the brick wall around the kitchen garden at Chartwell as well as building a swimming pool and goldfish pond.

When the news broke that WSC, then Chancellor of the Exchequer, was a part-time bricklayer, a local organizer of the Amalgamated Union of Building Trade Workers (AUBTW) wrote to him to enquire if he would like to join. After paying an admission fee of five shillings, WSC became a member on 10 October 1928. As he had been a strident opponent of the 1926 General Strike, many members of the AUBTW, which was affiliated with the Labour Party, demanded his expulsion. Eventually the Executive Council determined that he had been ineligible to join, and he was removed from the union.

SWIMMING AS STRESS RELIEF

While staying at the White House in December 1941, WSC suffered from a minor heart attack. He recuperated in January 1942 in Palm Beach, Florida, making sure the visit and health troubles were kept from the press. Walter Thompson, WSC's bodyguard, asked him if he wanted a bathing suit. WSC replied that because his villa opened directly onto the beach, he would not require one as he could simply step out of his room and walk to the water naked. As no other properties were close by, there was no chance of anyone seeing him. Thompson recalled that he was a very strong swimmer, keen on flipping around in the water like a 'porpoise'. After WSC was done swimming, he emerged from the waves and his bodyguard and valet wrapped him in a towel.

After the war in Europe had finished, WSC went on a week's holiday in south-western France in July 1945, to await the result of the General Election (it was delayed because ballots from soldiers serving abroad had to be sent in and counted). He stayed near Hendaye at the Château Bordaberry, which was owned by Raymond Brutinel, a Canadian entrepreneur who had stayed in France throughout the war. As well as painting, WSC enjoyed swimming, floating 'like a hippo' in the water. For security he was surrounded by a cordon of French policemen who had donned swimsuits (as did, presumably, WSC).

✌ The Chartwell Pool

At WSC's country residence there was a flood-lit outdoor circular pool that was kept heated year-round to a temperature of 75 degrees Fahrenheit (24 degrees Celsius); this necessitated a boiler about the same size as the one used to heat the House of Commons.

CHURCHILLIAN CINEMA

When WSC stayed at Chequers for the weekend during the Second World War, there was usually a movie shown every night. His favourite was Sir Alexander Korda's 1941 historical drama *Lady Hamilton* (also known as *That Hamilton Woman*), which WSC watched seventeen times, often being moved to tears by it. The film told the story of Emma Hamilton, an actress who became the mistress of Admiral Horatio Nelson. Vivien Leigh starred as Hamilton while Laurence Olivier played Nelson. The film so moved WSC because it was set at a time when Britain was facing down a vast European empire bent on its destruction – something that resonated with his war-time struggle. Another hit with WSC was *'Pimpernel' Smith*, in which Leslie Howard played the title character who rescued inmates from POW camps in Nazi Germany.

Of course WSC has been portrayed by many notable actors. The very first was the Scotsman C. M. Hallard, who appeared as WSC in the 1935 film *Royal Cavalcade*, which depicted the key events of George V's reign. Other notable actors to play WSC include Richard Burton, Albert Finney, Bob Hoskins, Christian Slater, Brendan Gleeson, Timothy Spall, Michael Gambon, John Lithgow, Brian Cox and Gary Oldman (who won the Oscar for best actor in 2018 for his performance in *Darkest Hour*). Clemmie has also featured in media, and been played by the likes of Vanessa Redgrave, Miranda Richardson and Kristin Scott Thomas.

MUSIC

WSC's preferred musical choices were military band tunes, popular vaudeville numbers, Gilbert and Sullivan musicals, and school songs from his Harrow days. During the Second World War, his favourite songs included 'Keep Right on to the End of the Road' by Sir Harry Lauder and 'Run, Rabbit, Run' by Noel Gay and Ralph Butler. WSC also enjoyed singing Music Hall songs dating back to his youth such as 'Daddy Wouldn't Buy Me a Bow-wow' and 'Ta-ra-ra Boom-de-ay'. After his retirement as Prime Minister in 1955 he developed more highbrow tastes, learning to appreciate the works of Brahms, Mozart and Beethoven.

WAR-TIME LITERATURE

Understandably, WSC did not have much time for recreational reading during the Second World War. However, when he travelled to Newfoundland in August 1941 he devoured the first three books in the Horatio Hornblower series by C. S. Forester, which tells the story of a fictional Royal Navy officer's exploits in the Napoleonic Wars. It had been recommended to him by his colleague in the War Cabinet Oliver Lyttelton, the Minister for the Middle East. The other handful of books WSC is known to have read while war-time leader were older ones he was very familiar with; while he was recovering from a bout of pneumonia in December 1943 his daughter Sarah read him Jane Austen's *Pride and Prejudice*, and in September 1944 he read Austen's *Emma* as well as Anthony Trollope's *Phineas Finn* and *The Duke's Children*.

✌ Impromptu Recitals

According to his private secretary, WSC, when he was in the company of close friends or family and the conversation flagged or the topic bored him, would often begin to recite poetry aloud. Favourite poets included William Shakespeare, Alexander Pope, Algernon Charles Swinburne or Thomas Babington Macaulay. Not all of the poems he recited were by great masters; a consistent favourite was from an edition of *Punch* and concerned ducks in St James's Park.

CHAPTER 5

Libations and Victuals

THE ORIGIN OF THE UBIQUITOUS CIGAR

WSC's tobacco habit started early; he began smoking cigarettes in 1890, while still at Harrow. His mother Jennie was not pleased, as his father, Lord Randolph, was plagued with health problems because of his heavy smoking (this did not stop him sending his son a case of cigarettes while he was at Sandhurst). Within a few years WSC had found a new source of tobacco: his famed cigars. This time, both parents disapproved of them.

According to his valet Norman McGowan, WSC smoked about nine cigars a day, although he usually did not finish them, leaving the ends in ashtrays (he instructed that they be saved and given to his gardener to smoke in his pipe). When he smoked a cigar, WSC liked to warm the tip with a candle and then wrap a piece of gummed brown paper (he called them his 'bellybandoes') around the other end. As he enjoyed chewing on cigars, this device prevented them from getting too wet. It also limited his direct intake of nicotine. To light cigars he used a long match so that the taste of sulphur could burn off from it before he applied the flame to the cigar; he tended to use two-inch-long matches made of Canadian cedar-wood. WSC usually kept between three and four thousand cigars in his house; however, many of them were gifts.

While he often smoked a cheaper American cigar called a Royal Derby Longfellow, his favourite smokes were the larger, more expensive Cuban brands, particularly Romeo y Julieta and Aroma de Cuba. This love of Cuban cigars began in 1895, when he travelled to the country to observe the War of Independence there.

✌ An Unusual Cigar Box

In 1945 WSC was given a gift from the people of Leningrad
(present-day St Petersburg). The box could hold 100 cigars and
was decorated with a brass plate featuring the flags of the United
Kingdom and Soviet Union. Inside the lid was a portrait of WSC
made from tobacco leaves.

WHISKY AND WINSTON

WSC's drinking habit has been over-stated; although he
certainly imbibed alcohol regularly (particularly by
today's standards), he was considered a 'sipper' rather than a
'guzzler', and was blessed with a sturdy constitution. His usual
tipple was whisky, for which he had developed a taste when
serving in the North-West Frontier Province in 1897. At the time,
whisky was not in fashion in England and on the few occasions
WSC had tried it he had not enjoyed the smoky taste. However, as
whisky was the only drink available, WSC learned to appreciate
it by the end of the campaign.

WSC even had time for a whisky when he was on the run from
the Boers in 1899. While being sheltered by the helpful English
colliery manager mentioned earlier, WSC helped himself to a
whisky and soda, served alongside a cold leg of mutton. That
night WSC hid down a mine, where he was provisioned with
roast chicken, a box of candles, cigars and, of course, a bottle
of whisky.

✌ Mouthwash

WSC mostly drank blends rather than single malts and was particularly partial to Johnnie Walker black or red label. He drank it without ice and heavily diluted with water or soda. It was so weak that this beverage was described as his 'mouthwash'.

PRIORITY PROVISIONS

When WSC sailed to South Africa in 1899 on the RMS *Dunottar Castle* to work as a war correspondent, he had sixty bottles of alcohol in his baggage, which had been purchased from the wine merchant Randolph Payne of Pall Mall. Considering he was scheduled to be there for four months, his order was relatively modest:

    18 × St Emilion claret (36 shillings)
      6 × port (21 shillings)
      6 × French vermouth (18 shillings)
    18 × ten-year-old Scotch (72 shillings)
      6 × Vin d'Ay Sec champagne, 1889 vintage (54 shillings)
      6 × eau de vie, 1866 vintage (75 shillings)

Also included were a dozen bottles of Rose's lime juice cordial.

✌ A Drinking Wager

While on holiday in Morocco in the winter of 1935–6, WSC bumped into the famed newspaper magnate Viscount Rothermere, who bet him £2,000 that he could not forgo alcohol for the whole of 1936. WSC refused to take the wager but did accept one for £600 that he would not drink brandy or undiluted spirits. History does not record if he was successful.

CHAMPAGNE

There is no doubt that WSC's favourite beverage was champagne, which he tended to drink out of a silver tankard. From 1908 his champagne house of choice was Pol Roger. In 1944 he befriended its owner, Odette Pol-Roger, who sent him a case of his preferred 1928 vintage for his birthday every year until it ran out in 1953. In return WSC named one of his racehorses after her. When WSC died, black borders were placed around the labels on Pol Roger bottles, and they named their most prestigious vintage the *Cuvée Sir Winston Churchill*.

THE COST OF THE HIGH LIFE

Throughout his life WSC was keen to be a good host and ensured the liquor cabinet and wine cellars at his homes were well stocked. In 1935, for example, he spent about 6 per cent of his disposable income on alcohol, and the bill with his supplier, Raymond Payne, came to £515 (this added up to around

£10 per week, three times an average manual worker's weekly wages). Over half of WSC's drink budget went on champagne, around one-third was for spirits, 10 per cent for port and sherry, and the rest went on claret, white wine and hock.

✌ Frontline Fare

When he served on the Western Front in 1916, WSC made sure he was well provisioned. He received food boxes from Fortnum & Mason, corned beef, stilton, cream, ham, sardines, dried fruit, steak pie, peach brandy and other liqueurs. He also brought a gramophone to put in the officers' mess.

THE PRIME MINISTER'S COOK

WSC's personal cook from 1939 was Mrs Georgina Landemare. She had been married to the French chef at the Ritz Hotel (he had died seven years previously). She prepared all of the meals WSC ate at home. He loved her cooking; some of his favourites included sole in a creamy white wine sauce with prawns, beef tenderloins with foie gras and black truffles, and even the occasional curry. He also liked classic British dishes like roast beef and Yorkshire pudding, and jugged hare. Landemare carried on working for the Churchills until she retired fifteen years later. In 1958, encouraged by Clemmie, she published *Recipes from No. 10*, which recorded the dishes she had cooked for WSC.

NO TEA FOR THE PRIME MINISTER

W ar-time rationing and shortages meant people had to take condensed milk in their tea. As WSC detested condensed milk he simply swapped his breakfast tea for a glass of sweet German white wine. This lack of tea was no great loss; at breakfast WSC enjoyed coffee or orange juice (although he liked the latter bottled rather than freshly squeezed). Another breakfast staple which did not feature on WSC's table was marmalade; he preferred black cherry jam with tinned pineapple.

✌ The Churchillian Sandwich

WSC had strong opinions on sandwiches; he believed the bread should be sliced wafer-thin, just thick enough to carry the filling.

DIPLOMATIC DINING

T he talks between WSC and FDR, held in August 1941 off the coast of Newfoundland in Canada, were crucial to the future of British and Allied success in the Second World War. Although the USA would not enter the war until that December, the meetings saw it declare its support for the Allies and established the close personal friendship between WSC and FDR that would be so vital over the next four years.

For WSC, no detail was too small when it came to planning the talks – even what was on the menu. On the first day of talks, 9 August, dinner was held on the USS *Augusta*; the American menu featured vegetable purée, broiled spring chicken, spinach omelette, candied sweet potatoes, mushroom gravy and chocolate ice-cream. WSC wanted the British-hosted banquet, held the next day on the HMS *Prince of Wales*, to be both seasonal and demonstrative of their national cuisine.

He did make a slight exception: the starter of smoked salmon was accompanied by Russian caviar (it had been provided as a gift from Joseph Stalin to Harry Hopkins, who had recently been in the USSR and had travelled across the Atlantic with the British flotilla). Turtle soup, a traditional Royal Navy dish since the eighteenth century, was next. A live turtle had been impossible to procure in war-time London, but WSC's aide-de-camp Tommy Thompson had been able to find turtle soup for sale in a grocer's in Piccadilly and was able to purchase enough for the banquet because it was not rationed. The main course was roasted grouse, personally bagged in Scotland by the Minister of Information, Duff Cooper (although the hunting season for the bird traditionally began on 12 August, it had been moved forward because of rationing). Furthermore, a dozen brace of grouse had been frozen and were given to FDR as a gift. The American President reciprocated with a present to be distributed among the British seamen: 1,500 boxes, each containing an orange, two apples, 200 cigarettes and half a pound of cheese.

✌ Favourite Pudding

When it came to dessert WSC preferred to order off-menu if possible; his habitual choice was Roquefort cheese, a peeled pear and ice-cream.

DIPLOMATIC DINING II

In August 1942 WSC travelled to the Soviet Union for meetings with Stalin in Moscow. At the conference there was a state banquet held at the Kremlin. The menu was staggering in its richness and scale, particularly given that there were long bread lines across the country. The meal started with cold hors-d'oeuvres: caviar, salmon, sturgeon, garnished herrings, dried herrings, cold ham, game mayonnaise, duck, soused sturgeon, tomato salad, salad, cucumber, radishes, cheese. Hot hors-d'oeuvres followed: white mushrooms in sour cream, forcemeat (ground meat) of game, eggplant *meunier*. There was more to come: *crème de poularde*, borsch, sturgeon in champagne, roasted poultry, potato purée, lamb with potatoes, cucumber salad (with more caviar) and asparagus. To finish there was ice-cream and fruit ices, coffee and liqueurs, fruit, petits fours and roast almonds. The dinner lasted three hours, and was accompanied by lots of wines and twenty-five toasts given by Stalin.

DIPLOMATIC DINING III

At the 1945 Yalta Conference an even more elaborate dinner was held. It started with caviar, pies, a selection of fish, cold piglet, game broth and cream of chicken soup. This was followed by a selection of dishes including grilled skewers of baby lamb, tenderloin of veal, quail, baby partridges and black-tailed gazelle. The food concluded with a concoction called the *Churchely* (or 'Churchills'), a sweet Georgian nut dish that resembled a long cigar. As was traditional, there were toasts throughout. The Soviet Minister of Foreign Affairs, Vyacheslav Molotov, served as the *tamada* ('toastmaster'). Unfortunately, the speeches interfered with the serving of the food, so it was cold when it arrived. In total there were forty-five toasts; to stay sober most people watered down their champagne or poured vodka into potted plants. For Stalin's final great toast to the grand alliance a specially selected Armenian brandy was served. The dinner finally ended at 12.45 a.m.

✌ A Slice and a Twist

At Yalta the Soviets had taken great care to ensure the comfort of their distinguished guests by importing lemon trees from the other side of the Black Sea so that WSC could have a slice in his G&T and FDR could have a twist in his martini.

A DEDICATED BON VIVEUR

In 1944, following a tour of Italy, WSC developed a sudden fever of 103 degrees Fahrenheit (39 degrees Celsius). He then travelled across the Atlantic on the *Queen Mary* to attend the Second Quebec Conference. Despite being on antibiotics and antimalarials, he ate richly; one meal included oysters, consommé, turbot, roast turkey, ices with cantaloupe, stilton with fruits and petit fours. This repast was washed down with Mumm champagne (1929 vintage), Liebfraumilch and brandy from 1870.

RATIONING

For most of his life WSC was able to eat whatever he liked. One of the few exceptions was when he was imprisoned at a POW camp in Pretoria in 1899, during which time his daily ration was half a pound of beef (tinned or fresh), bread, potatoes and tea. Forty years later, while the rest of the country was subject to strict war-time rationing, WSC mostly continued his usual diet (he was also subject to rationing but could supplement his supplies with produce from his Chartwell estate).

Rationing continued in the United Kingdom even after the fighting had finished in 1945. When WSC returned to power in 1951 one of his first aims was to end rationing, but shortages meant that he actually had to cut the meat ration. Harold Macmillan, the Housing Minister and future Prime Minister, claimed that when WSC was shown an adult's weekly meat ration he thought it was just for a day, and stated it would make one perfectly good meal. Happily for the country, WSC's government was able to end rationing in 1954.

✌ A Heavyweight

In 1954 WSC was over fifteen stone (95 kilograms). To help him lose weight Clemmie put him on a diet mainly consisting of tomatoes, which WSC did not enjoy.

CHAPTER 6

Winston's Menagerie

CAMELS

While WSC was Colonial Secretary he visited Egypt for the 1921 Cairo Conference. In the midst of the discussions about the future of the Middle East, WSC had time for a two-and-a-half-hour camel trek to the Sphinx with a party that included Clemmie, his bodyguard Walter Thompson, the writer and archaeologist Gertrude Bell and T. E. Lawrence. More used to horses, WSC had some trouble handling the camel, but galloped along nonetheless. According to Thompson he then fell off the camel. WSC was uninjured and insisted on continuing the journey on camel despite being offered a horse. After reaching the Sphinx he declined the chance to take a car back and once again took to his camel, accompanied by Lawrence and Thompson.

✌ A Bulldog for a Bulldog

At age seventeen, while at Harrow, WSC sold his bicycle to purchase a bulldog named Dodo.

WINSTON THE LEPIDOPTERIST

WSC was fascinated with butterflies; at age six he wrote to his mother saying he loved collecting them. He continued the practice in India, but, alas, his specimens were destroyed by a rat (which was eaten by his terrier, unimaginatively also named Winston). Later in life, WSC wanted to breed butterflies at Chartwell and called in a local expert L. Hugh Newman to help him. A game larder was converted into a butterfly house, and Newman and WSC introduced several rare species, including foreign ones. The programme was not a roaring success: his gardeners mistakenly cut down plants where caterpillars were breeding, and WSC lost interest in the project.

BLACK SWANS

In 1927 WSC's friend Sir Philip Sassoon, a Liberal politician and art collector, gave him a pair of black swans. They lived at Chartwell, and in 1949 they were joined by four more black swans that were gifted to WSC by Sir James Mitchell, the Governor of Western Australia (the birds appear on the state's badge and coat of arms). Native to Australasia, the black swans found life in the comparatively chilly Chartwell hard and also faced attacks from local foxes. In 1954 one went missing; it was eventually recovered 240 miles away in Uden, a small town in the Netherlands, and returned. To this day, there are still black swans living at Chartwell.

MARMALADE MOGGIES

There were always cats at Chartwell while WSC lived there; two of his favourites were a tabby called Mickey and a marmalade-coloured one called Tango. Tango was particularly close to WSC; he often slept on his bed and joined him at his table for mealtimes. WSC would clean Tango's eyes with a napkin and feed him mutton as well as sometimes practising speeches in front of him.

For WSC's eighty-eighth birthday one of his private secretaries Sir Jock Colville gave him a marmalade cat. WSC adored the cat, which he named Jock, and it travelled with him between Chartwell and his London residence, sometimes lying on the backseat of his car. The Churchills requested that there always be a marmalade cat with a white bib and socks residing in Chartwell and living a comfortable life. Since the National Trust took over Chartwell in 1966 they have always honoured this wish. In 2014 the latest marmalade cat, a seven-month-old rescue kitten called Jock VI, moved in.

✌ Conquering Nelson

WSC also kept a cat at 10 Downing Street, a big grey called Nelson brought over from the Admiralty. WSC had adopted the cat after seeing it chase a large dog away. Admiring his courage, he had named it after Britain's greatest admiral and given it a home. When the Churchills moved into 10 Downing Street there was already a cat resident, which became known as the 'Munich Mouser' because it had been associated with Neville Chamberlain's administration. At first the two cats lived together, but eventually Nelson chased away the previous feline occupant.

RUFUS THE POODLE

One of WSC's closest companions was a tan-coloured miniature poodle called Rufus. He ate with the rest of the Churchill family in the dining room; his bowl was placed on a cloth that was laid next to the head of the table. No one else ate until the dog had finished. Sadly, Rufus died in 1947 at the Conservative Party's conference in Brighton, when he was run over by a bus after one of WSC's maids let the dog off his lead. Rufus had become such a popular side-kick to WSC that *Life* magazine stepped in to purchase a similar dog for £40 from the same kennels – it was named Rufus II. WSC loved his new dog just as much. While watching the film adaptation of *Oliver Twist*, when it came to the scene where Bill Sikes drowned his dog WSC covered the eyes of the little poodle, who was sitting on his lap. Rufus II lived until he was fifteen years old and died in his sleep in 1962. However, he was never fully house-trained, and often left unpleasant surprises on the floor.

✌ Tears for a Donkey

When it came to animals WSC was unashamedly sentimental; he was moved to tears by the death of any of his pets. This compassion extended to fictional beasts, such as the one featured in the 1951 film *Never Take No for an Answer*, which tells the story of an Italian war orphan called Peppino and his faithful donkey Violetta. When Violetta sickens, Peppino travels across Italy, all the way to the Pope in Rome, to get permission to take his donkey to the shrine of St Francis of Assisi for healing. The movie was screened for WSC. Whenever the camera cut to the ailing donkey lying ill in his stable, WSC said he would not continue to watch if the animal died. Fortunately, Peppino persuaded the Pope to let the donkey enter the shrine, and he was restored to full health. When the film ended, WSC's cheeks were moist with tears.

CHURCHILL'S LION

In 1938 a businessman called George Thomson took ownership of a lion (according to rumours, after winning a bet). As Thomson was the managing director of a firm called Rotaprint, he named the lion 'Rota', and it lived in the back garden of his house in the London suburb of Pinner. Thomson's neighbours were not greatly enamoured of a lion living in their area, particularly during the Blitz, when it was feared a stray bomb might break open Rota's cage and set him loose. On 29 May 1940 Thomson finally gave his lion to London Zoo because, due to rationing, he could no longer feed him enough meat. In 1943 London Zoo presented WSC with the lion to commemorate recent Allied successes in North Africa. Thankfully it did not come to live in 10 Downing Street but remained in the zoo. WSC, on his wartime walks through London, often strolled from Westminster to Regent's Park to see Rota.

The lion, which had grown fairly tame in its years in captivity, became something of a celebrity and featured in four films. After Rota died in 1955 at the age of seventeen he was stuffed and eventually found his way to St Augustine, Florida, where he is displayed at the Lightner Museum of antiquities and curiosities.

THE PLATYPUS

While he was busy turning the tide of the war, WSC had time to indulge his passion for exotic animals. A particular fascination was for the rare and unusual Australian animal the platypus. As a live specimen had never been seen in Europe, in March 1943 he wrote to the Australian Prime Minister John Curtin requesting six platypuses. Although it was illegal to export the species from Australia, Curtin made an exception. While preparations were being made, WSC was sent a stuffed platypus called Splash, which he placed on his desk. The Healesville Sanctuary in Victoria was charged with preparing six platypuses for transport; its director David Fleay (who had bred the first platypus in captivity) informed both governments that this was an impossible task and that only one could be sent. A male platypus, named Winston, was chosen for the long voyage to Britain. Winston was to be housed at London Zoo, and the keepers there exchanged numerous telegrams with Australia discussing how to build the best 'platypussary' for him. The staff at London Zoo also planned an elaborate publicity campaign for the platypus, which included an appeal to the public to send in worms to feed their newest animal.

The platypus's ship, the MV *Port Phillip*, left Melbourne in September 1943 and arrived in Liverpool, via the Panama Canal, in November. On its voyage it was cared for and fed by a ship's cadet. Unfortunately, the platypus died four days before it reached Britain. It was probably as a result of shock and disruptions to its environment caused by a submarine attack. By this time the platypus may have been weakened; it was supposed to eat 750 worms a day, but because the ship had had to take a longer route its ration had been cut to less than 600. The platypus was stuffed and was initially supposed to be given to the Royal College of Surgeons to replace one they had lost in the Blitz. However, its location and ultimate end is not known.

Although the enterprise shows WSC's whimsy, it also had practical implications; a live platypus would have been a nice distraction for London's battered population as well as an important subject of zoological research. Most importantly the exhibition of the platypus would help build and solidify cultural bonds between Britain and Australia, and reflect the alliance between the two nations.

✌ Digger the Kangaroo

One of WSC's most unusual gifts was a rare white kangaroo named Digger (Australian and New Zealand slang for a soldier) given to him by the Australian Stockbreeders' Association. He considered having him live at Chartwell, but ultimately decided that London Zoo would be a better home.

THE BUDGIE

One of WSC's closest companions in his later years was a yellow budgerigar called Toby, who would sit on the rim of his spectacles, peck his cigars and hop across his desk as he worked. When WSC travelled to France, Toby would join him. Unfortunately, in February 1961 Toby was lost after flying out of an open window of WSC's room at the Hôtel de Paris in Monte Carlo. Despite his offering a reward of £22 for the bird, it was never recovered. Heartbroken, WSC never got another budgie.

A PARLIAMENTARY LADYBIRD

Whenever an insect flew into his rooms, WSC would insist it should not be killed, but put gently out of a window. This courtesy to the insect world extended to Parliament. Once, during the 1950s, when the MPs were filing out of the Commons, the Conservative Secretary of State for War, Anthony Head, spotted a ladybird on the floor. As the tiny beetle was in danger of being trampled, Head picked it up. Having witnessed the incident, WSC told him to release it out of a window – however, due to the air conditioning system, this was locked. Head then set off to find a window that did open. Later that day Head stopped by WSC's office, briefly interrupting a meeting with the French foreign minister, to tell him that the ladybird had been safely set free.

WINSTON'S HERD

As well as being WSC's country residence, Chartwell was also a farm. Among the earliest residents were dairy cows and Middle White pigs (of which WSC was particularly fond). Mary and Sarah, WSC's daughters, kept bantams, which were allowed to wander around the house and pecked up food from the dining room floor. Later on, a herd of goats arrived. The farming at Chartwell was initially difficult, partly because the Churchills often grew too fond of the animals and became reluctant to slaughter them.

Eventually, the farm thrived, particularly the cows. The first herd were Belted Galloways, a Scottish breed with a long black coat and a broad white belt that encircles the body. They were a gift from Sir Ian Hamilton, who WSC had served with in the Second Boer War (later he had been the commander of the expeditionary force that had landed at Gallipoli in 1915). There were also shorthorn cattle at Chartwell; in 1949 one of them, 'Gratwicke Beatrice 2nd', won a competition at Tunbridge Wells, netting a £10 prize.

THE RACEHORSE OWNER

L ord Randolph had been a fairly successful horse owner, and after the Second World War WSC followed his father's example. Encouraged and advised by his son-in-law Christopher Soames, WSC began to purchase horses in 1949. They raced under his father's old colours of pink with chocolate sleeves and cap. The first, and most famous, member of WSC's stable was Colonist II, a French-bred grey thoroughbred he purchased for £1,500 in 1949. He won thirteen of the twenty-four races he entered, including the Jockey Club Cup, winning over £12,000 in prize money. One of his victories was at the Winston Churchill Stakes, run at Hurst Park in Surrey, which WSC personally watched with Princess Elizabeth (her father also had a horse in the race – a black filly called Above Board who Colonist II beat into second place). After the 1951 season Colonist II was sold to stud at auction for £7,350. Over the next fifteen years WSC would own many other horses (in total thirty-six racehorses and twelve brood mares); they won a combined total of seventy races.

🐟 Fishy Friends

The ponds at Chartwell were stocked with goldfish and huge Golden Orfe that WSC liked to feed; the fish would swim towards him when he tapped his cane against the flagstones.

CHAPTER 7

The (Right) Honourable Member

THE FIRST SPEECH

The first political speech WSC made was on 26 July 1897 addressing a fete held for the Primrose League, an organization set up in 1883 to popularize Conservative principles. Lord Randolph had been one of the leading figures in its establishment and WSC's mother, Jennie, served on its first Ladies' Committee. The meeting was held at Claverton Manor near Bath, and WSC (home from India on leave) spoke about the Workmen's Compensation Bill and 'Tory Democracy'.

THE IMPORTANCE OF PREP

WSC never employed a speech-writer. He dictated speeches to a secretary, who would type them out for him on strips of paper so he could re-arrange and re-jig the content, and jot down notations. He would then refer to these papers while speaking. WSC's thorough preparations dated back to an incident that occurred when he was still a backbench Conservative MP. On 22 April 1904 he was making a speech, which he had learned off by heart, in a Commons debate about trade unions. After forty-five minutes he stalled on the phrase 'it rests with those who'. He stood for three minutes, but, without notes and unable to regain his train of thought, eventually sat down in silence and buried his head in his hands to the sound of jeering from some of the other MPs.

✌ Tips of the Trade

WSC always had strong opinions about oratory; in 1897 he wrote an essay entitled 'The Scaffolding of Rhetoric'. It argued that short, Anglo-Saxon words were more impactful than long ones of Latin or Greek origin. Furthermore, it asserted that the speaker should have a poetic rhythm, evoke a succession of vivid images and not be afraid to appeal to emotion.

OLDHAM: THE FIRST CAMPAIGN

In 1899 WSC began a campaign of networking and public speaking in a bid to win a nomination to stand for election to Parliament. An opportunity arose in the north-western town of Oldham, where the Conservatives held two seats (at the time, some constituencies had two MPs). A by-election was called after one of its MPs died of pneumonia and the other, who was chronically ill, resigned. On 23 June, WSC was officially selected as one of the Conservative candidates. The other was a markedly different figure: James Mawdsley, a trade unionist who had started work in a cotton mill at the age of nine. They were running against two Liberals: Alfred Emmott, the owner of a local cotton spinning firm who had previously been mayor, and Walter Runciman, the son of a shipping magnate. Polling day was 6 July. WSC was unsuccessful; he finished in third place, trailing behind both Liberals. WSC would be a candidate at twenty more parliamentary elections. He lost just four of them.

1900: VICTORY IN OLDHAM

Now a celebrity, following his escapades in South Africa, WSC returned to Oldham on 25 July 1900. He was met by cheering crowds and regaled a large audience at the town's theatre with tales of his escape from Boer captivity (coincidentally, one of the English miners who had helped him while he was on the run was Dan Dewsnap, an Oldham native). When the local Conservative Association asked WSC to run again in Oldham, he agreed.

Prime Minister Salisbury dissolved Parliament on 26 September. The ensuing General Election took place against the background of a tide of patriotism inspired by the Second Boer War (as such it is also called the Khaki Election, for the colour of British Army uniforms), which would sweep the Conservatives to a landslide victory. WSC took campaigning in Oldham very seriously; he was joined by his mother and Sir Joseph Chamberlain, an influential Conservative whose public endorsement was a major coup. WSC's Conservative running-mate was a stockbroker called Charles Crisp (Mawdsley, whom WSC had run with in 1899, had retired from public life after his china bathtub shattered under his weight, causing serious injuries). WSC and Crisp were running against the incumbent Liberal MPs, Emmott and Runciman.

On 1 October the Oldham results were declared. Emmott retained his seat and held it until 1911, when he was raised to the House of Lords. In second place was WSC; at just twenty-five he was an MP.

✌ Lord Runciman and the Betrayal of Czechoslovakia

The man WSC had dislodged, Runciman, returned to Parliament in 1902, rising to become President of the Board of Trade, and in 1937 was raised further to the peerage. In 1938 Runciman led a diplomatic mission to Czechoslovakia to resolve the dispute between its government and the ethnic Germans in the Sudetenland region of the country. His report recommended that the Sudetenland be transferred to Germany. This paved the way to the infamous Munich Agreement, where Europe's great powers yielded to Hitler's demands and unilaterally allowed Germany to annexe parts of Czechoslovakia.

THE YOUNG MP

....

Due to his lecture tour of the UK and North America, WSC did not take his seat in the Commons until 14 February 1901. He made his maiden speech four days later, on the subject of the ongoing war in South Africa. He called for the conflict to be brought to a swift end by cutting off pockets of resistance. Watched from the Lady's Gallery by his mother and aunts, he urged the government to be just and not punitive or vengeful against the Boers. Reports on the speech were generally favourable, although they mentioned that WSC looked like a young scholar rather than a soldier, as well as pointing out the trouble he had with pronouncing the letter 's'.

CROSSING THE FLOOR

Ultimately, WSC found his early years as an MP depressing; he was frustrated with his lack of power and was moving politically away from the Conservatives towards the Liberals. The main point of contention arose because many Conservatives, led by Joseph Chamberlain, were calling for tariffs to protect British manufacturing from foreign competition. As WSC was a supporter of free trade, this drove a wedge between him and his party, and led to WSC making a momentous decision: he would abandon the party of his father and grandfather.

WSC 'crossed the floor' on 31 May 1904 and sat down next to the leading Liberal David Lloyd George on the opposition benches. It was the exact same seat his father, Lord Randolph, had occupied when he waved off William Gladstone with a handkerchief after he resigned as Prime Minister in June 1885. For his action Conservatives nicknamed WSC the 'Blenheim Rat'.

✌ Wax Winston

After WSC's crossing of the floor, Madame Tussauds added a waxwork statue of him to their collection.

COLONIAL TOUR

In December 1905 WSC became a junior minister, taking up the post of Under-Secretary of State for the Colonies. Two months later he faced a General Election. As WSC had been deselected by the local Conservative Association in Oldham, he had to find a new constituency. He was selected to contest the nearby seat of Manchester North West. As part of the Liberal landslide victory, WSC won his seat by over a thousand votes, meaning he retained his post in the Colonial Office. As part of his official duties, WSC undertook a tour of British colonial possessions in the Mediterranean and East Africa from 1907 to 1908. After holidaying in Venice he boarded the HMS *Venus*, a Royal Navy cruiser, which took him via Aden in Yemen to Mombasa in Kenya. WSC, accompanied by 350 porters, travelled inland towards Lake Victoria. Although it was an official trip, WSC spent a lot of time hunting the local wildlife; his kills included zebra, wildebeest, gazelle and a rhinoceros. The expedition then travelled to Lake Victoria and followed the White Nile north by train and steamboat. In Khartoum WSC's valet George Scrivings died of choleraic diarrhoea having eaten some tainted food. After reaching Cairo, WSC went on to London, arriving in January 1908, having travelled over nine thousand miles. Nine articles about the voyage appeared in *Strand Magazine*. They formed the bulk of a book, *My African Journey*, published that November. It included sixty-one photographs, some of which WSC may have taken himself.

MILITARY OBSERVATION

In September 1906 WSC travelled to Silesia (a region now mostly in Poland but then part of Germany) and spent a week observing the manoeuvres of the Imperial German Army. He stayed in Breslau (now Wrocław) and with other guests and officials was taken by train out to the countryside to view the assembled ranks of 50,000 soldiers going through their exercises. The evenings were spent at official banquets and WSC even met Kaiser Wilhelm II. WSC reported that the Germans were well organized and disciplined, although he noted that Wilhelm had little conception of the power of modern weaponry. In September 1909 WSC returned to Germany to observe their army's annual manoeuvres a second time. This time he travelled to Bavaria, staying at Würzburg and again meeting the Kaiser.

PRESIDENT OF THE BOARD OF TRADE

On 3 April 1908 Campbell-Bannerman resigned due to ill health (he died of a heart attack nineteen days later). The new Prime Minister was Asquith, with whose daughter, Violet, WSC was close friends. As part of the reshuffle, WSC was promoted to President of the Board of Trade – at just thirty-three he had his first ministerial post. Under parliamentary rules at the time, a newly appointed Cabinet minister had to seek re-election from his constituency. They were normally allowed to run unopposed, but because of WSC's crossing of the floor, the Conservatives ran a candidate against him. WSC lost the Manchester North West by-election on 24 April. The Liberals quickly found a vacant seat for him – Dundee in Scotland – which WSC duly won on 9 May.

THE ULTIMATE PENALTY

In February 1910 WSC was appointed Home Secretary. This doubled his annual salary to £5,000 and made him one of the most senior figures in the government. One of his most important duties was to sign the death warrants of people sentenced to execution. The first was for Joseph Wren, an unemployed former sailor living in Lancashire. He had cut the throat of a three-and-a-half-year-old girl. On 21 February, a few days after he took up the post, WSC reviewed the case and did not issue a reprieve. The man was hanged the next day at Strangeways Prison in Manchester. While he was Home Secretary, WSC had to review forty-one more death cases, authorizing a reprieve on twenty occasions.

✌ Crippen

One of the men whose sentence WSC did uphold was Dr Crippen, who was found guilty of poisoning and dismembering his wife. He was hanged on 23 November 1910.

THE SIEGE OF SIDNEY STREET

On the morning of 3 January 1911 WSC was having one of his customary baths at his London home when he was informed of an armed stand-off between the police and two Latvian anarchists, Fritz Svaars and William Sokoloff, at 100 Sidney Street in Stepney, East London. The two men were wanted in connection with a gang that had robbed a jeweller's, killing three policemen. The police had traced the men to Sidney Street and while they slept had cleared the area of civilians and cordoned it off. They had then evacuated the other residents from the building where the two anarchists were holed up. At 7.30 a.m. the gunfire started; Svaars and Sokoloff were both well armed and had ample ammunition. More firepower was needed to contain the situation, so at around 9 a.m. the police contacted the Home Office to ask for permission to call in a detachment of riflemen from the Scots Guard who were based at the Tower of London. WSC, as Home Secretary, was then asked to give permission to do this, which he duly did.

The riflemen arrived at Sidney Street at 10 a.m. and the shooting continued. WSC, eager to see the events in person, was on the scene by lunchtime, wearing a silk hat and an astrakhan coat. By 1.30 p.m. a fire had started at the house. WSC, who until now had been an observer, intervened to prevent the London Fire Brigade from putting out the blaze – telling their commanding officer to let the house burn down and only step in if the conflagration spread (he was unable to stop a dedicated postman from delivering letters to the house next door). By 2.30 p.m. the shooting had stopped; the firemen were then allowed to begin extinguishing the fire. Both Svaars and Sokoloff had died in the blaze.

✌ Caught on Camera

Also at the scene were cameras from Pathé News; WSC, in his top hat, was conspicuous in the newsreel footage. He was criticized for rushing to the scene and accused of being an interfering grandstander. When the newsreels of the siege were screened, many cinema-goers booed when WSC appeared. The public ill-will continued into the summer; on 22 June at George V's coronation, WSC's carriage was booed by the assembled crowds.

WINSTON AND THE SUFFRAGETTES

A s a young politician WSC opposed women being given the vote, although he was by no means the most strident critic of female enfranchisement (in contrast, his wife Clemmie was a supporter of the cause). Due to WSC's high profile, he was the target of many suffragette campaigners. In 1905 Emmeline Pankhurst was imprisoned after disrupting a speech WSC was making at the Manchester Free Trade Hall. Suffragette disruption continued while he was campaigning in the 1908 Manchester North West by-election. He addressed crowds standing atop his limousine, but his speeches were interrupted by heckling and shouts of 'Votes for women!' Later that year, in the Dundee by-election, WSC was followed around by Mary Maloney, an Irish suffragette. She carried a placard saying 'Votes for women' and rang a bell to drown out WSC when he spoke.

Encouraged by Clemmie, WSC later moderated his views and began to support the gradual extension of the vote to women. However, he believed that enfranchising them all at once would be too disruptive. He supported the 1918 Representation of the People Act that gave the vote to all men over twenty-one and women over thirty who held £5-worth of property – but it was not until ten years later that *all* women over twenty-one could vote.

✌ Whipped into Submission

On 14 November 1909 WSC was attacked at Bristol Temple Meads railway station by a suffragette called Theresa Garnett. Brandishing a whip, she forced him back towards the train tracks, before she was pulled away by policemen (some reports say it was Clemmie who did this). Garnett was given a month in prison for disturbing the peace. As WSC was leaving the station another woman threw an iron bolt at his car and he was punched by a male supporter of the suffragettes. The windows of the Churchill house in London were often smashed, and after their daughter Diana was born, her pram had to be guarded because of concerns she would be kidnapped.

THE FIRST LORD OF THE ADMIRALTY

Since the early seventeenth century the First Lord of the Admiralty was responsible for directing and advising the government on naval affairs. Asquith appointed WSC to the position in October 1911 (offering him the job while they were golfing together in Scotland). It was an important post; the Royal Navy was one of the pillars of British imperial strength. WSC devoted himself to the job, largely ignoring domestic affairs. His mission: to modernize the Royal Navy. One of his main policies was to champion the use of oil to power ships, rather than coal. To secure the UK's oil supply, in 1913 he pressed the government to buy a controlling interest in the Anglo-Persian Oil Company (later renamed British Petroleum). WSC also urged the Navy to invest in research and development of aerial power – this was around the time he was learning to fly.

THE ENCHANTRESS

One of the perks of being First Lord of the Admiralty was the use of the official yacht HMS *Enchantress*, a twin-propeller vessel with a crew of 196, built in 1903. WSC made his first visit on 5 November 1911, coming aboard at Cowes on the Isle of Wight (where his parents Randolph and Jennie had met). He loved life aboard the *Enchantress*, and it became his second office. In the three years before war broke out in 1914, WSC spent a combined total of eight months on board (often joined by friends and family), visiting almost every vessel, port, shipyard and naval facility in the waters around Britain.

WSC also toured the Mediterranean on the *Enchantress*. The purpose of these cruises was to inspect British naval bases, but there was also time for leisure. In 1912, joined by Asquith and his daughter Violet, WSC visited southern Italy, viewing Mount Vesuvius and the Temple of Zeus in Paestum (where he became obsessed with catching the green gecko lizards that scurried about the site). The outbreak of the First World War put a stop to these useful (and pleasurable) trips on the *Enchantress*. Its crew was sent to serve on the battlecruiser HMS *Invincible*, which was sunk at the Battle of Jutland in 1916. Meanwhile, the *Enchantress* was converted into a hospital and was ultimately sold for scrappage in 1935.

✌ Fishy Business

In 1913, WSC, Clemmie and the Asquiths visited Malta, Sicily and Corsica. During that trip, there was a fishing expedition; WSC found traditional methods too slow so used depth charges to stun the fish. He then engaged fifty sailors to trawl the waters with a large net.

THROWING THE BOOK AT WINSTON

In the midst of a November 1912 debate on Irish Home Rule, the situation got so heated and raucous that the House of Commons had to be adjourned. As the Opposition left the Chamber they threw wadded-up paper at the government benches. WSC responded, rather provocatively, by waving a handkerchief at them. Enraged, Ronald McNeill, a six-foot six-inch Ulster-Scot, threw the Speaker's copy of the Standing Orders of the House at him. It hit him in the face, drawing blood (some sources say it only caused serious bruising). WSC had to be restrained from charging at McNeill, who was nearly a foot taller than him. The next day calmer heads prevailed; McNeill apologized and both WSC and the House of Commons accepted it.

THE FALL OF ANTWERP

On 4 August 1914 the British government declared war on Germany, plunging the nation into a four-year conflict that would become known as the Great War. Although WSC stated that it would be 'business as usual' for the British people, it soon became clear that this was a war of an unprecedented scale and ferocity. Fighting on the Western Front, which ran through Belgium and France from the North Sea coast to the Swiss border, descended into a boggy morass. Both sides had dug in, creating an elaborate system of fortified trenches.

WSC's first major involvement in the war ended in failure. On 28 September 1914 German forces began to bombard Antwerp, whose extensive port on the Scheldt Estuary made it one of the most important strategic targets in Europe. Although it was heavily fortified, German forces appeared poised to break through and capture the city. On 2 October, King Albert I of Belgium informed his British and French allies (whose promised reinforcements had not arrived) that he would be unable to hold Antwerp and planned to evacuate to prevent his army being trapped. The next day WSC personally visited to persuade the Belgians to hold out as long as possible. To help out, a detachment of Royal Marines were rushed to the city, arriving on requisitioned London buses. Their presence was not enough. From 8 to 9 October, Belgian and British forces began to evacuate Antwerp, which formally surrendered to the German commander the next day.

GALLIPOLI

With the Western Front a stalemate, WSC proposed opening a new front. The Allies would invade Turkey via the Dardanelles Strait, a narrow channel that separated Europe from Asia. Controlling it would allow Britain and France to send supplies to Russia as well as divert German and Austro-Hungarian forces. The Allied leadership approved the plan and the Mediterranean Expeditionary Force was raised. It would be commanded by WSC's old friend from the Second Boer War General Sir Ian Hamilton and include soldiers from Australia, New Zealand, Britain and France (later joined by reinforcements from India and Newfoundland). WSC and the rest of the Allied leadership underestimated Turkish strength and resolve. The fighting quickly became as deadlocked as on the Western Front, except played out under the baking Mediterranean sun. One of the few successes was that some Allied submarines snuck through the Dardanelles and attacked Turkish shipping around Istanbul. Allied land forces were finally evacuated in January 1916. Over 50,000 had been killed. Nothing had been gained.

There was plenty of blame to go round for the tragic failure, but WSC bore the brunt of it. In May 1915 he resigned as First Lord of the Admiralty. He remained in the Cabinet, but his new position was the Chancellor of the Duchy of Lancaster, a sinecure post with little power or influence.

WINSTON'S TANKS

In February 1915 WSC established the Landships Committee, charging them with developing some kind of armoured vehicle to break through the German trenches. He was partly inspired by H. G. Wells's description of armed iron-clad 'land-ships' in a 1903 short story. The committee continued after WSC's resignation from the Admiralty, and in September 1916 the first tanks were used in combat on the Western Front. By the end of the war they were being utilized with increasing success by both Britain and France (although the Germans developed tanks, their effectiveness lagged behind those of the Allies).

During the Second World War, the British Churchill tank was named after WSC. When France was defeated, it was rushed into service in 1941. Unfortunately, the tank suffered from many faults: its engine was slow and unreliable, and its armament was weak. These early setbacks were eventually remedied, and the Churchill proved to be an effective and versatile tank. It was used in Western Europe, North Africa and Italy, and a few hundred were even sent to the Red Army for use on the Eastern Front. Before the British Army phased it out in 1952, the Churchill was also used in the Korean War.

ON THE FRONTLINE

WSC resigned as Chancellor of the Duchy of Lancaster in November 1915 and returned to the Army as a major. In December he went to the Western Front for one month of training with the Grenadier Guards infantry regiment. By the new year he was a (temporary) lieutenant-colonel commanding the sixth battalion of the Royal Scots Fusiliers, posted at Ploegsteert (known as 'Plug Street' by the British) in Flanders, a fairly quiet sector at the time. WSC's second-in-command was Archibald Sinclair, who later became a close friend and led the Liberal Party from 1935 to 1945.

WSC was popular with his men, explaining duties to sentries and pointing out good positions to fire on the enemy without being hit. While on the front, he made thirty-six forays into No Man's Land, placing himself at some risk. He was caring and attentive to wounded soldiers but perhaps over-lenient on disciplinary matters, and always chatty with other officers, perfectly willing to discuss the failures of Antwerp and the Dardanelles as well as gossip about figures such as Kitchener and Asquith (neither of whom he was particularly complimentary of).

With little chance of a promotion or a transfer to a more active sector, WSC returned home in March. After he left, his battalion was involved in the 1916 Somme Offensive as well as the Battle of Passchendaele (1917). In Parliament WSC was highly critical of Asquith's leadership – as were others. In December 1916 the Conservatives in the National Coalition ministry resigned, leaving Asquith's position untenable. After Asquith resigned, Lloyd George formed a new coalition government, although initially he did not invite WSC to serve as a minister.

✌ Priorities, Priorities

As leader of the battalion, WSC's first major initiative was a campaign of delousing, as well as encouraging sports days and singing while marching. He then focused on building and repairing the trenches at which his battalion was stationed.

RETURN TO PROMINENCE

In July 1917 WSC returned to the Cabinet as Minister of Munitions, putting him in charge of ensuring the country's supply of ammunition was sufficient to fight, and win, the war. In November 1918 the Great War finally came to an end, although conflict continued elsewhere. In the aftermath of the 1917 October Revolution, the Russian Civil War (1917–22) had broken out. WSC promoted (direct and indirect) British involvement in the war on the side of the anti-communist White Army. The UK was also involved in the Irish War of Independence (1919–21), which saw British security forces fight a guerrilla campaign against Irish republicans. WSC was a hard-liner who was instrumental in the decision to send in the 'Black and Tans', a paramilitary force of former soldiers who became infamous for their brutality. By summer 1921 the conflict had hit a stalemate, and both sides came to the negotiating table; WSC was one of the signatories of the resulting Anglo-Irish Treaty, which ended the war and gave Ireland self-government and eventually independence (the six counties that make up Northern Ireland opted out and remained part of the United Kingdom). Another area of concern was the Middle East, which had been carved up into French and British spheres of influence. In Iraq, which was a British mandate, WSC pressed for the use of airpower to retain control of the region and suppress uprisings from Kurdish tribesmen.

A SURPRISE AT THE RITZ

In 1919 WSC travelled to Paris for the signing of the Treaty of Versailles (which he was largely uninvolved in negotiating – the likes of Lloyd George, US President Woodrow Wilson and French Prime Minister Georges Clemenceau played far more of a role in determining its terms). While staying at the Ritz Hotel, WSC was introduced to another guest Daisy Decazes de Glücksberg, a twenty-nine-year-old socialite who was the daughter of a German duke and also a member of the Singer Family, who had made a fortune manufacturing sewing machines. Daisy was a divorcee; her first marriage had ended after she allegedly caught her husband, a French aristocrat, in bed with his male chauffeur. Daisy invited WSC up to her room to meet her young daughter. However, when he entered he found Daisy reclining nude on a chaise-longue, lying on a tiger-skin. WSC left at once. The next year Daisy married WSC's cousin the banker Reggie Fellowes. Despite this incident, Daisy became good friends with both WSC and Clemmie.

✌ The Loss of an Appendix (and Dundee)

The November 1922 General Election was disastrous for WSC and the Liberal Party. The Conservatives won a majority and Andrew Bonar Law became Prime Minister (due to throat cancer he resigned the following May and was replaced by Stanley Baldwin, the Chancellor of the Exchequer). WSC suffered from an attack of appendicitis while campaigning in Dundee, and had to have his appendix removed. He was forced into fourth place.

THE OILMAN

In the summer of 1923, WSC, no longer an MP, was engaged in writing his history of the First World War. As he had recently purchased Chartwell, which needed major repairs, he was a little short of cash. Help arrived from the oil industry. Royal Dutch Shell and Burmah Oil wanted to merge with the Anglo-Persian Oil Company, of which the British government was the majority shareholder. For £5,000 (worth over £260,000 today) WSC was hired to persuade Baldwin to sell the government's controlling shares. Before the deal could go through, a General Election was called in November 1923, ending WSC's brief career as an oil lobbyist.

CHANCELLOR OF THE EXCHEQUER

In the October 1924 General Election WSC returned to Parliament after winning Epping, a constituency in Essex on the outskirts of London. The Conservatives won the election and Baldwin asked WSC to take up the crucial post of Chancellor, putting him in charge of the nation's finances. WSC formally re-joined the Conservatives and remained in the party for the rest of his life. The most controversial issue of WSC's chancellorship was his decision to return the UK to the Gold Standard. This meant that from 1925 the value of the pound was tied to the value of gold, because notes could be converted to bullion. This was supposed to bring stability and add confidence to the economy. However, WSC had set the pound at its pre-war rate, which by now was incredibly out of date. British goods became far too expensive for foreign markets, leading to falling demand for exports. This led to a decline in manufacturing and coal-mining, deflation and high unemployment (the Gold Standard was finally abandoned in 1931). It also contributed to the May 1926 General Strike, which saw 1.7 million workers walk out over a nine-day period. WSC was hostile to the strikers, and edited the *British Gazette*, a short-lived anti-strike propaganda newspaper published by the government from 5 to 13 May, reaching a circulation of two million. In the May 1929 General Election, the Conservatives, and WSC, were voted out of office.

NORTH AMERICAN TOURS

From August to October 1929 WSC travelled around North America to promote *The Aftermath*, the fourth volume of his history of the First World War. Although he was no longer in government, WSC was still received at the White House, where he met President Herbert Hoover. This trip also saw WSC's only sojourn to the West Coast, where he visited the newspaper baron William Randolph Hearst at his lavish mansion in San Simeon, California. WSC was less than complimentary of Hearst, describing him as a 'grave simple child' with a bad temper. Shortly before he left, the Wall Street Crash struck; an event that left WSC's finances in a parlous state.

In December 1931 WSC again left England for an American lecture tour. His first stop was New York but disaster struck the day after his first lecture. He had had dinner with Clemmie at the Waldorf-Astoria and then travelled up-town to meet his friend Bernard Baruch, a financier and philanthropist, who lived just off Fifth Avenue. WSC did not have the exact address but was sure he could find Baruch's residence once he was in the neighbourhood. As he was looking around he stepped out onto Fifth Avenue and was struck by a car travelling at thirty miles per hour. WSC was hit on the forehead and cracked two ribs. He had to spend a week in hospital and the next month convalescing in the Bahamas. While he was recuperating, he developed pleurisy, and the accident left WSC with lingering pain in his arms and shoulders.

Despite the seriousness of the accident, WSC carried on his work. He had been hired to write about his trip for the *Daily Mail* and continued to file copy – even receiving an increased fee because public interest had risen as a result of the crash. On 28 January 1932 he resumed his tour in Brooklyn before spending the next month speaking across the USA as well as making an appearance in Toronto. WSC's itinerary took in several major cities, including Pittsburgh, Cleveland, Detroit, Cincinnati, Indianapolis, Chicago, St Louis, Minneapolis, New Orleans, Atlanta and Washington DC. He earned more on this tour than he did in a year as an MP. His next visit to the USA was nearly a decade later, as a Prime Minister visiting a war-time ally.

✌ Welcome Home, Winston!

The Churchills returned home in March 1932. While WSC was gone a group of friends and well-wishers had raised £2,000 to buy him a Daimler motor-car as a welcome-back gift. The donors included the press magnates Lord Beaverbrook and Lord Camrose, the former Foreign Secretary Edward Grey, the future

Prime Minister Harold Macmillan, the Prince of Wales (later Edward VIII), the economist John Maynard Keynes and even Charlie Chaplin.

THE WILDERNESS YEARS

For most of the 1930s WSC devoted himself to writing and painting. This was not wholly his choice. Although still an MP, he was increasingly alienated from his party, particularly over the issue of Indian independence, which he would not countenance. In 1936, during the Abdication Crisis, he was also supportive of a compromise solution that would have let Edward VIII stay on the throne.

Recognizing the threat posed by the fascist regimes in Italy and Germany, WSC's greatest cause was arguing for re-armament and against appeasement. His appeals were mostly ignored. By 1937 he was probably at his lowest ebb. He was mostly regarded as being washed-up, and had few allies in Parliament. Everything changed in 1938. The increasing bellicosity of Nazi Germany, and their annexation of Austria and Czechoslovakia, proved WSC's dire warnings were correct, and made him a relevant and vital figure once more. When war broke out in September 1939, WSC returned to government as First Lord of the Admiralty; his greatest deeds were to come.

CHAPTER 8

The Churchill Look

THE DANDY

As a youngster WSC customarily sported a shirt with a starched-wing collar, frock coat and watch chain. He completed the look with a glossy top hat. Even during the 1930s and 40s, WSC retained some features of the Edwardian style such as the three-piece suit, polka-dot bow tie, pocket square and Homburg hat. He did so because he thought it was essential for public figures to have a distinctive look.

✌ A Cruel Nickname

WSC's nickname at Harrow was 'Copperknob', for his reddish hair. He was also mocked on account of his stutter and slight lisp. His diminutive stature did not help; WSC's height (as recorded in his file at Sandhurst) peaked at just under five foot seven inches.

THE PRIVY COUNCILLOR

The Privy Council is a body of advisors to the British monarch, made up of senior politicians; membership is for life and carries with it the right to be styled 'The Right Honourable'. WSC became a privy councillor in 1907. On ceremonial court occasions he wore its formal uniform of a dark tailcoat decorated with gold embroidery, white breeches and stockings, and a cocked hat with an ostrich-feather plume.

✌ Facial Hair

For almost all of his life WSC was clean-shaven. The only exception came in South Africa, when he grew an almost invisible moustache.

A SARTORIAL FAILURE

Clemmie and WSC's 1908 wedding was one of the social events of the year but his suit attracted some criticism. *Tailor and Cutter* magazine noted that it looked like it had been flung together at the last minute and made him look like a 'glorified coachman'.

THE SEAFARER

As First Lord of the Admiralty WSC adopted a maritime look, wearing a navy-blue double-breasted suit with the white cap of the Royal Yacht Squadron. When he met FDR at Placentia Bay he wore the undress uniform of an Elder Brother of Trinity House, which consisted of a navy-blue suit with two rows of gold buttons topped with a matching cap. Trinity House is a fraternity dating back to 1514 concerned with maritime safety as well as acting as a charity for sailors; WSC had been made an honorary Elder Brother when he became First Lord of the Admiralty. His other maritime uniform was the one he gained through holding the ceremonial office of Lord Warden of the Cinque Ports (a group of five coastal towns in south-east England) from 1941 to

1965. The uniform is modelled on that of a Royal Navy admiral, and features gold and red trim decorated with the Cinque Ports insignia, a bicorne hat and a light-blue sash.

A *CHAPEAU* FOR LIEUTENANT-COLONEL CHURCHILL

While serving on the Western Front with the Royal Scots Fusiliers, WSC wore the light-blue ornamental helmet of the *poilu* (a French infantryman) because he did not care for his regiment's traditional Glengarry bonnet (although he did wear it for an official group photograph). From time to time he would don it and look at himself in a mirror before chuckling, swearing and taking it off.

✌ A Father's Robes

When Stanley Baldwin made WSC Chancellor of the Exchequer in 1924, there was no need to make him the traditional robes of that office. Rather, WSC simply took out of storage the robes that his father, Chancellor in 1886, had worn.

ACADEMIC ROBES

Although he never attended university, WSC was awarded twenty-one honorary degrees, from academic institutions across the world. They included Queens University Belfast, Harvard, McGill in Montreal, the University of Copenhagen,

Leiden University, the University of Oslo and the University of London, as well as an honorary professorship at Massachusetts Institute of Technology.

WSC held a variety of senior academic offices. From 1914 to 1918 he was Rector of the University of Aberdeen and from 1929 to 1932 he held the same post at the University of Edinburgh. The longest association he had with a university was with Bristol; he served as its Chancellor from 1929 to 1965. WSC was a surprising choice for the office; in 1929 he had just lost the position of Chancellor of the Exchequer, and his career was regarded as waning. However, he was very popular with students, and after his installation ceremony he was wildly cheered and carried through Bristol on their shoulders. On official occasions he wore the Chancellor's academic robes, which were made of black satin richly patterned with gold.

✌ A College to Call Your Own

In addition to his academic honours, WSC was heavily involved in the founding of Churchill College, Cambridge. The college was announced in 1958 and was the first in Cambridge to be named after a living person. To raise the funds needed to build it (£3.5 million – over £75 million today) a charitable appeal was announced. WSC headed the board of trustees and the physicist Sir John Cockcroft, who had won the Nobel Prize in Physics for splitting the atom, was named as its first master. The site of the college was selected in 1959, and WSC visited to plant two trees. The first buildings were completed in 1960, and the first students arrived that year. The college is the home of the Churchill Archives Centre, which houses WSC's papers.

CHURCHILL IN COSTUME

WSC had a life-long fascination with Middle Eastern culture, and in private would sometimes dress in Arab-style robes with his friend the poet and writer Wilfred Blunt. WSC also had a life-long interest in the Muslim religion, and in 1940 his government set aside £100,000 for the building of London Central Mosque to appeal to Arab and Muslim nations.

UNDERCLOTHES

WSC would only wear silk underclothes. They were pale pink and during the Second World War he purchased them from the Army & Navy Store, at the cost of around £80 per annum. He said the fabric was essential because of his delicate skin. A particularly sensitive area was a patch on his right forearm from which flesh had been scalpelled to graft onto the arm of a fellow soldier Lieutenant Richard Molyneaux while they were on campaign in the North-West Frontier Province in 1897. Apart from a patch of eczema on his jaw, WSC had very smooth skin. He achieved this through liberal use of a skin cream called Lait Larola made by M. Beetham and Son of Cheltenham.

✌ Dressing Gowns

As WSC spent hours every day in bed or getting in and out of baths, dressing gowns were an essential feature of his wardrobe. He favoured silk gowns, usually brightly coloured and embroidered with dragons or flowers. One of his favourites was a particularly vibrant number originally designed to be worn by the character of Pooh-Bah in the Gilbert & Sullivan comic opera *The Mikado*. To complete the look he wore slippers monogrammed with his initials.

THE SIREN SUIT

WSC's most comfortable and utilitarian war-time outfit was his siren suit, also referred to as his 'romper'. It was a zip-up one-piece designed by WSC personally. It had large pockets, a belted waist and was loose enough to be put on over other clothing. It came in several styles; there was a heavy wool version in Air Force blue, a lightweight model for tropical weather, as well as mauve, bottle-green velvet and grey pinstriped versions.

COMMODORE AND COLONEL

On 4 April 1939 WSC was made an Honorary Air Commodore of No. 615 (County of Surrey) Squadron, part of the Auxiliary Air Force. He wore the office's pale blue uniform on many occasions, for example during the 1943 Tehran Conference. In 1947 WSC was being awarded the Médaille militaire at a ceremony in Paris. He planned to wear his air commodore's uniform but Clemmie advised him not to, saying it would not be suitable for him to wear a military outfit. WSC promised that he would wear civilian clothes, but in the end it was reported he did wear another of his uniforms for the ceremony, that of the Fourth Hussars, his first regiment. He had been made its honorary colonel in 1941. During the Second World War, the Fourth Hussars, which had long been converted from a cavalry force to an armoured regiment, fought in Greece, North Africa and Italy. In 1943, while they both happened to be in Cyprus, WSC took time from his one-day visit to the island to address and inspect the regiment. As a result of amalgamations in the British Army, the Fourth Hussars no longer exists; it is now part of the Queen's Royal Hussars, which has served in both Iraq and Afghanistan.

CHAPTER 9

Never Surrendering, Always Inspiring

THE ROAD TO WAR

In March 1939 Germany invaded Czechoslovakia. The country was erased from the map; the western part was annexed by Germany and the Slovak Republic, a Nazi client state, was established in the east. The Germans followed this by invading Poland on 1 September. Two days later, after their ultimatum to Germany to withdraw from Poland was ignored, the UK and France declared war, followed by the Commonwealth nations of New Zealand, Australia, South Africa and Canada. The outbreak of war led to WSC's return to political prominence. Neville Chamberlain, Prime Minister since 1937, named WSC as First Lord of the Admiralty and a member of his nine-man War Cabinet.

The day war was declared air-raid sirens went off in London. WSC, still living at his flat in Morpeth Mansions, initially did not go down to the local air-raid shelter. He was persuaded to do so to set a good example – before he left he made sure to grab a bottle of brandy.

TOMMY THOMPSON

Charles Thompson (known as Tommy) had served in the submarine service in the First World War, and in 1936 was named Flag Lieutenant (essentially aide-de-camp) to the First Lord of the Admiralty. When WSC was re-appointed to the office in 1939, he and Thompson got on well. After WSC became Prime Minister he requested Thompson join him, and in July 1940 he was officially attached to his staff. Throughout the war Thompson was almost always by WSC's side at home and abroad.

✌ The American Connection

On 11 September 1939 FDR wrote the first of many messages to WSC. They would eventually exchange over 1,700 letters and telegrams. While he was First Lord of the Admiralty, WSC signed off as 'Naval Person'. After he became Prime Minister he switched to 'Former Naval Person'.

MD1: CHURCHILL'S 'TOYSHOP'

One of WSC's initiatives was Operation Royal Marine, a plan to float mines down rivers from France into Germany, where they would destroy infrastructure and water transports. The French were unwilling to allow this, as they were concerned it would further provoke Germany. The plan was only put into place after 10 May 1940, when Germany had launched its invasion of France. Although the mines had some limited success, they did little to stop the German onslaught.

The mines were developed at Ministry of Defence 1 ('MD1'), a secret research and development organization. WSC saw its value and ensured MD1 was given adequate funding and facilities. They returned his confidence with a range of useful inventions, including the sticky bomb, limpet mine and the 'PIAT' (Projector, Infantry, Anti Tank – a handheld weapon that could take down tanks).

THE END OF CHAMBERLAIN

On 7 May 1940 a debate in the Commons on the conduct of the war began. Chamberlain's leadership was roundly criticized from both sides of the House. The next day a vote of confidence in the government was held. Chamberlain won by 281 votes to 200, but many in his own party voted against him. Chamberlain tried to shore up his position by forming a coalition government. On 9 May Labour leaders informed him that they were willing to join a coalition, but indicated that they would not feel comfortable serving under Chamberlain. A meeting followed between WSC, Halifax, Chamberlain and David Margesson, the Conservative Chief Whip. They discussed who would succeed Chamberlain if he resigned. The precise details of their conversation are shrouded in mystery, but Halifax (the favoured candidate of both Chamberlain and George VI) is said to have stated he could not lead the country from the House of Lords. This left WSC.

At dawn the next morning, news reached London that Germany had attacked the Low Countries, the prelude to the invasion of France. Chamberlain contemplated continuing as leader but Attlee reasserted that Labour would not serve under him. At 5 p.m. the Labour leadership confirmed that they were willing to join a coalition led by WSC. Chamberlain then went to Buckingham Palace and resigned as Prime Minister (although he remained Leader of the Conservative Party), recommending WSC to succeed him. George VI sent for WSC and requested he form a government. WSC formally became Prime Minister at 6 p.m. At this stressful time he was without Clemmie. His brother-in-law, Colonel Bertram Romilly, had died on 6 May in

Herefordshire. As a result Clemmie had to leave London with her sister Nellie to make funeral arrangements.

WINSTON'S WAR CABINET

A fter WSC became Prime Minister he named himself Minister of Defence, and gave cabinet posts to politicians from the Conservative, Labour and Liberal Parties. The core leadership was a streamlined five-man War Cabinet. Its membership never exceeded nine people, which ensured the body could act efficiently.

✌ Tap, Tap, Tap

During Cabinet meetings, WSC habitually tapped on the arm of his chair with his signet ring finger, which, as the war progressed, wore away several layers of lacquer.

THE CHURCHILL WAR ROOMS

S ince the 1920s there had been plans to build a secure bunker for British government leadership so that it could remain in Westminster even if it came under enemy aerial attack. In June 1938 a site was chosen: the basement of the New Public Offices building, located near Parliament and 10 Downing Street. The Cabinet War Rooms were created by reinforcing the basement and installing telecommunications equipment. The complex was declared operational on 27 August 1939. The nerve-centre was the Map Room, where reports and information were collected by the armed forces to give an instant strategic overview. There was also the Cabinet Room, where WSC hosted 115 War Cabinet meetings. WSC also had an office-bedroom down there. Although he used it for napping, he only stayed overnight there three times because he did not like sleeping underground. The facility remained operational non-stop until 16 August 1945.

✌ Quiet Please

WSC could not abide distractions. To ensure quiet in the Cabinet War Rooms, several Remington Noiseless typewriters were imported from the USA for the secretarial staff.

WINSTON AND FRANCE

There was no foreign country that WSC spent more time in than France. His first visit was in the summer of 1883 with his father. While in Paris they observed the monuments at the Place de la Concorde covered in wreaths and mourning rags to mark the loss of the provinces of Alsace and Lorraine to Germany after the Franco-Prussian War. WSC's French was fairly basic, but he had a deep knowledge of the country's history and greatly admired Joan of Arc and Napoleon.

In the weeks after he became Prime Minister, WSC made five

visits to France in a desperate attempt to help the nation survive the onslaught of the invading German forces. On 15 May, Paul Reynaud, French Prime Minister since March, telephoned WSC telling him that France was beaten. The next day WSC flew to Paris for crisis talks. The situation was dire; the French Army had no reserves left and the Luftwaffe enjoyed aerial superiority. Still, France agreed to fight on and not make a separate peace with Germany. When WSC returned to France on 22 May, the situation appeared more positive. WSC met Maxine Weygand, the new commander-in-chief of the French Army, at his headquarters outside of Paris. Weygand outlined his ambitious plan for a counterattack that would see British and French forces link up to drive the Germans back. But when WSC returned to Paris on 31 May, the situation had not improved; some Allied troops had been cut off at Dunkirk and their evacuation was ongoing. Regardless, WSC told the French that Britain would fight on.

WSC again met Reynaud on 11–12 June. As Paris was about to fall, the French leadership had withdrawn 100 miles south to a chateau near the town of Briare. There was a final meeting between WSC and Reynaud on 13 June. WSC's aeroplane had set out without him knowing where the French cabinet was. Eventually he was told they could be found in the city of Tours, which was swamped by thousands of refugees. After WSC located Reynaud they had lunch together, and both parted with tears in their eyes. On the return flight, WSC's aeroplane had to dive suddenly when a German Heinkel was spotted. Fortunately for them it was busy strafing a French fishing boat and so did not spot the Prime Minister's aeroplane. On board, WSC asked his bodyguard Thompson for his Colt .45, saying he did not want to be taken alive if they were shot down.

✌ A Trusty Pug

Hastings Ismay, nicknamed 'Pug', was WSC's chief military assistant and the intermediary between him and the armed forces. His diligence as an administrator and skill as a mediator were vital. As WSC insisted on brevity in papers sent to him, Ismay developed the ability to boil down complex matters to their essentials (he was allowed to attach lettered appendices; on one particularly lengthy report he got all the way to the letter T).

CABINET IN CRISIS

By late May German forces had overrun most of France. Over 300,000 Allied soldiers had been forced back to Dunkirk, where they were surrounded by German forces. They faced the prospect of annihilation or capture. On 26 May, Operation Dynamo, the heroic evacuation of the stranded men, began. It was completed on 4 June.

On 27 May a War Cabinet meeting was held. Halifax believed a military victory was impossible, and suggested that they approach Mussolini (at this stage Italy was still neutral) to serve as a mediator for a peace deal with Germany. Halifax threatened to resign if WSC did not consider negotiation – something that could have shattered confidence in his nascent term as Prime Minister. The next day WSC addressed his entire cabinet. Would he tell them mediation would be sought or that Britain would fight on? WSC chose the latter course. Following an inspirational address, all of the ministers present cheered; it was clear the country's leadership were firmly behind WSC.

✌ Sawyers

WSC could devote himself entirely to the war effort because he had a team of servants who catered to his every need. Leading them was his butler and valet, Frank Sawyers, entrusted with intimate tasks such as laying out WSC's clothes, preparing his baths and helping him to dress. Sawyers left WSC's service after the war. In his 1945 Resignation Honours list, WSC awarded him the Defence Medal for his work. Unlike many of the great man's other confidantes, Sawyers rarely spoke publicly about his personal experiences with him.

CHEQUERS

WSC spent many weekends at Chequers, the Buckinghamshire country house of the Prime Minister. He welcomed friends, family and hundreds of other guests but was always joined by his aide-de-camp Tommy Thompson, his bodyguard Walter Thompson, Sawyers, three secretaries, an electrical engineer, two film operators, three chauffeurs, a detective and a large group of policemen. Despite the change in venue, WSC's nocturnal habits continued. Dinner usually finished at 10 p.m., and was followed by a film that ended at midnight. WSC and his guests would then work or converse until about 2.30 a.m., when the household would finally retire.

WAR-TIME ROUTINE

When he was not travelling, WSC would wake up at 8 a.m. and go through the newspapers in bed. He then worked until around 1 p.m., before having his first bath and a shave (with an electric razor). He then dressed, lunched and worked for another hour. It was then time for his afternoon nap (usually taken nude), during which he covered his eyes with a black satin eye-mask. After he woke up, he had another bath followed by dinner. He would then work until the early hours, often up to 4 a.m.

✌ Ploughing Through Paperwork

Each day, WSC worked his way through mountains of reports, correspondence and memoranda. They were all placed in a box with the most pressing paperwork kept in a special subdivision known as 'top of the box', which was for matters that had to be solved immediately. To facilitate efficiency, WSC had special red labels made up that read 'action this day'. This tag meant that he wanted the issue to be resolved as soon as possible.

MISSION TO MOSCOW

Operation Barbarossa, the Axis invasion of the USSR, was launched on 22 June 1941. Soviet forces were completely unprepared; even though Joseph Stalin had been warned about it dozens of times, he refused to believe it would happen. This changed the course of the war, bringing the USSR into the conflict on the Allied side. It was not always an easy alliance. WSC had supported the anti-Bolshevik forces during the Russian Civil War and had opposed communism his entire political career.

From 12 to 17 August 1942, WSC travelled to Moscow via Gibraltar and Cairo for his first face-to-face meeting with Stalin (codenamed Operation Bracelet). At this stage Axis forces controlled most of Stalingrad and were driving towards the vital Baku oilfields. As such, it was a delicate time for the Allies. WSC disappointed Stalin by informing him that the Western Allies would not be opening a second front in Europe that year by invading France. This cast a pall over the proceedings until, on the evening of the last day, WSC requested a private talk with Stalin in his rooms (later joined by the foreign minister Vyacheslav Molotov and, presumably, some translators). Lubricated by vodka and red wine the leaders spoke until 3 a.m. This late-night drinking session helped WSC and Stalin to forge a working relationship, although they never developed a strong rapport. They both doubted each other's honesty and long-term aims, and WSC found Stalin to be stubborn and bad-mannered.

✌ Cigars at Altitude

During the war, WSC spent hundreds of hours on board aircraft. For the most part, conditions were Spartan; the cabins were chilly and there were sometimes only canvas bunks or mattresses on the floor to sleep on. The aeroplanes were unpressurized, which meant that WSC, who was susceptible to pneumonia, had to wear an oxygen mask, even while sleeping. He later had it modified with a hole that enabled him to smoke his cigars while still wearing the mask.

WINSTON AT THE WHITE HOUSE

On 7 December 1941 Japanese aircraft launched a surprise attack on the US naval base at Pearl Harbor, Hawaii. The next day the USA declared war on Japan. On 11 December both Germany and Italy (who were allied with Japan) declared war on the USA. The Arcadia Conference, held in Washington DC from 22 December 1941 to 14 January 1942, was the first full meeting of the US leadership with their new allies.

WSC, who had formed a close relationship with FDR through correspondence and their meeting at Newfoundland in August 1941, set out for the USA on 13 December 1941. Following a stormy voyage across the Atlantic, he landed on 22 December. That morning the First Lady, Eleanor Roosevelt, was informed that WSC would be staying for three weeks. This infuriated her, as she had been told the British leader would only be their guest for a few days.

WSC and FDR lunched together every day, and often stayed up late drinking and smoking cigars. On Christmas Eve WSC joined FDR at the lighting of the White House Christmas Tree. After attending church with FDR on Christmas Day, WSC prepared for his speech to a joint session of the US Congress the next day. His address mentioned his American heritage and was greeted with great cheers by the audience. That evening WSC watched *The Maltese Falcon* with FDR and the Canadian Prime Minister, Mackenzie King. Later that night WSC suffered a minor heart attack. Undaunted, he travelled by train to Ottawa to address the Canadian Parliament. On New Year's Day 1942 the Declaration of the United Nations was signed, which stated the Allied powers would fight the Axis until they were defeated and not make any separate peace deals. WSC then spent five days recovering in Florida before returning to Washington for the end of the talks. He left the USA on 14 January, flying home from Bermuda on a seaplane.

✌ A Demanding House Guest

While staying at the White House, WSC was nothing if not demanding. He had turned down the Lincoln Bedroom because the bed there was not large enough. Instead, he was installed in the Rose Suite; his staff turned one of the rooms into a strategy centre, hanging maps on the wall. White House staff were informed there was to be no talking outside of WSC's room or whistling in the corridor. He requested a tumbler of sherry in his room before breakfast, whisky and soda after lunch, and champagne and ninety-year-old brandy in the evenings.

LUXURY LINER

In June 1942 WSC returned to the USA for talks with FDR, flying both ways on a seaplane. When he returned to North America in May of the next year for the Trident Conference, where the Allies discussed the upcoming invasion of Sicily, he travelled by ship, taking the RMS *Queen Mary*. Built for the Cunard-White Star Line, it had gone into service in 1936 and held the record for the fastest passenger service across the Atlantic. After the war started it was requisitioned by the government. Its costly fittings were ripped out and the ship was converted into a troop transport, which could carry over 15,000 men. A few luxury cabins were preserved for distinguished guests such as WSC. En route there was a lifeboat drill; WSC insisted that his cabin have a machine gun mounted on it so that he could resist capture if the ship went down. He took his second trans-Atlantic voyage on the *Queen Mary* that August, when he travelled to Canada for the First Quebec Conference (codenamed 'Quadrant'). After the war the *Queen Mary* resumed civilian passenger service until it was retired in 1967. It is now permanently moored in Long Beach, California, as a museum, hotel and restaurant.

EUREKA!

Held from 28 November to 1 December 1943, the Tehran Conference was the first meeting of the 'Big Three': WSC, FDR and Stalin. It began two days after the end of the Cairo Conference, where FDR and WSC met Generalissimo Chiang Kai-shek, who was leading the fight against Japan in China. Codenamed 'Eureka', the talks at Tehran saw the leaders set their military and strategic goals, including a commitment from the Western Allies to open up a second front against Germany in Europe.

WSC celebrated his sixty-ninth birthday in Tehran with a dinner that went on until 2 a.m. Such hours were *de rigueur* for WSC and Stalin, but unusual for FDR, who rarely stayed up late. At the party Sawyers dashed around the room filling everyone's glasses for the numerous toasts. Stalin was so impressed that he toasted him twice. One of Stalin's toasts was interrupted when an English waiter tripped and spilt desserts over his interpreter. WSC was given a range of presents, including a silver coin dating back to 300 BCE from his daughter Sarah (his aide for the conference), a carpet from the Shah of Persia and an astrakhan hat from the assembled press corps.

✌ On Target

As the Allies were preparing for D-Day in summer 1944, WSC inspected American soldiers with Eisenhower and General Omar Bradley, commander of the US First Army. He took on both men at target practice using the American M1 carbine and tried his hand at firing a bazooka. This would have been a welcome diversion for WSC; following the failure of the amphibious landings in Gallipoli in 1916, he was plagued with worries about a repeat of the disaster at Normandy.

CHURCHILL'S EGG

During the war, WSC flew on a range of aircraft, including the de Havilland Flamingo, the Lockheed Lodestar, the Boeing 314 Clipper (a luxurious flying boat) and the Douglas C-47 Skytrain (the model was the workhorse of Allied aerial transportation and logged millions of miles). The first aircraft assigned specifically to WSC was the *Commando*, a version of the American Consolidated B-24 Liberator bomber adapted for passenger transport. Built in the USA, it was delivered to Scotland in July 1942 by Captain William Vanderkloot, an experienced American pilot who had volunteered to serve in the RAF. Vanderkloot and the *Commando* flew WSC on several trips over hostile territory, including to Moscow for meetings with Stalin in August 1942 and to Morocco for the January 1943 Casablanca Conference. The *Commando* was painted matte black to prevent enemies spotting it.

In mid-1943 WSC switched to a British aircraft, the Avro York. His one was named *Ascalon*, after the lance St George used to slay the dragon. It had more amenities than the *Commando*, with a telephone, bar and a heated toilet seat (although WSC thought it was too hot and had it disconnected). British researchers had ambitious plans to make the plane even more comfortable – they had designed a prototype aluminium 'egg' that could be pressurized, creating a large chamber in which WSC could work, sleep and even smoke without an oxygen mask. Unfortunately, it was far too big and heavy to fit in the fuselage, so it was never installed.

At the end of 1944, WSC was given an American Douglas C-54 Skymaster (the same model as the US President's craft, named the *Sacred Cow*). Contained within was a panelled conference room and sleeping accommodation for six. WSC had his own stateroom with a divan, easy chairs and a desk. The Skymaster flew him to France, Greece, Yalta and Potsdam. Clemmie also used the craft for her March 1945 journey to the USSR to tour facilities of the Russian Red Cross; since 1941 she had been the chair of the British Aid to Russia Fund, which raised nearly £8 million in donations from the British public.

✌ To Battle!

WSC could never resist being in the thick of the action and frequently had to be prevented from putting himself at undue risk. The closest he got to battle as Prime Minister was while visiting the front in Northern Italy. On 26 August 1944 he travelled to Pisa, fired a howitzer and picnicked while the Germans were just 500 yards away.

YALTA

Following the success of the Tehran Conference, WSC wanted to hold another meeting of the Big Three in September 1944. His preferred choice of venue was on the Cromarty Firth in Scotland, the site of a Royal Navy base. The time and date were unacceptable to Stalin, so somewhere in the Mediterranean was suggested. This was also rejected by Stalin, who claimed that his doctors had advised against long-distance travel (in reality he hated flying). The Soviet leadership proposed the Black Sea resort of Yalta in Crimea (perhaps not coincidentally it meant that Stalin, and the Soviet delegation, could stay at one of his favourite dachas, Yusupov Palace, located in the nearby town of Koreiz), which the Western Allies agreed to. The talks, codenamed 'Argonaut', were held from 4 to 11 February 1945.

Before Yalta, WSC and FDR attended the Malta Conference, where the final push into Germany was planned. They then flew direct to Saki Airfield in Crimea before driving five hours south to Yalta. On the trip WSC entertained himself by reciting Lord Byron's epic poem *Don Juan*. The conference was held at Livadia

Palace, a summer retreat built for the Russian imperial family, and the main point of discussion was the shape of post-war Europe. Most importantly, it was agreed that after the war Germany and Berlin would be split into British, American, French and Soviet occupation zones. Stalin promised he would hold free elections in Poland and declare war on Japan after Germany had surrendered.

While FDR and the Americans stayed at Livadia, WSC and the British delegation were housed five miles away at Vorontsov Palace. It had been built between 1828 and 1848, for the Russian general Prince Mikhail Vorontsov, and was designed by the English architect Edward Blore. Until spring 1944 it had been the headquarters for the German Field Marshal Erich von Manstein when the Axis held the area. On the wall of the dining room at the palace WSC saw paintings of his relatives; in 1808 his distant cousin the eleventh Earl of Pembroke (the grandson of the third Duke of Marlborough) had married a member of the Vorontsov family.

✌ The Last Meeting

In total WSC and FDR spent 120 days together. On 15 February 1945 they met in person for lunch aboard the USS *Quincy*, which was docked at Alexandria. The meeting lasted over two and a half hours, and the main topic of the discussion was atomic weapons. Less than two months later, FDR died after a massive cerebral haemorrhage.

RELIEF ON THE SIEGFRIED LINE

On 2 March 1945 WSC flew to Brussels with Clemmie, Field Marshal Alan Brooke and Ismay. There they met Mary Churchill, who was serving in an anti-aircraft battery in Belgium. The party then had a lavish lunch hosted by Air Marshal Arthur Coningham. Clemmie and Mary remained in Brussels while WSC, Brooke, Ismay and Coningham flew on to Eindhoven in the Netherlands for afternoon tea with Montgomery. The next morning WSC crossed into German territory. Accompanied by around twenty generals, he viewed the Siegfried Line, the chain of fortifications that was supposed to defend the Third Reich from invasion. WSC and his party lined up along the line and relieved themselves on it. The press photographers present agreed to the request not to capture the event for posterity. WSC then spent the next three days touring the front, even chalking 'A Present for Hitler' onto a shell.

✌ A Heavy Workload

As war-time Prime Minister, WSC regularly worked over 120 hours a week. By 1945 the strain was showing. In meetings, he often rambled and repeated himself. His old schoolmate from Harrow, the Secretary of State for India and Burma Leo Amery, noted that when WSC had an attack of laryngitis in March 1945, it sped up cabinet meetings considerably.

POTSDAM

The last East–West conference of the war was held at Potsdam, on the outskirts of Berlin, from 17 July to 2 August 1945. The meetings saw WSC's first introduction to FDR's successor as President, Harry Truman. The day before the talks formally started they gathered for a morning meeting at 11 a.m.; it was apparently the earliest WSC had got out of bed for a decade. That afternoon WSC, wearing a white safari suit, toured Berlin with Eden. They were driven to the Reich Chancellery and escorted through its ruins by Red Army soldiers. The subsequent discussions were far more fractious than earlier meetings of the Allied leadership. WSC rightly believed Stalin wanted to establish dominance over Eastern and Central Europe and install friendly puppet regimes. WSC left Potsdam halfway through proceedings, never to return. Due to his defeat in the 1945 General Election he was replaced by the new Labour Prime Minister, Attlee.

✌ Bad Dreams

After the failure of discussions about the future of Poland at Potsdam, WSC told his physician Charles Wilson that he had had a dream that he saw his own dead body under a white sheet on a table in an empty room. He recognized it as his because of the feet poking out from under the sheet.

A NEW CONSTITUENCY

WSC represented Epping in Parliament from 1924 to 1945, when, due to redistricting, the new constituency of Woodford was created from it. WSC then served as Woodford's MP for nineteen years, winning it five times (he was its only MP; in 1964 it became part of the new constituency of Wanstead and Woodford). On 31 October 1959 he spoke at the unveiling of a statue of him in Woodford, despite suffering a recent attack of dizziness that had left him unconscious – it was the last public speech he had been able to work on himself.

IKE AND WINSTON

In October 1951 the Conservatives won the General Election, meaning that WSC was an elected Prime Minister for the first time. In the USA a new President, Eisenhower, took office in January 1953. Although WSC thought Eisenhower had been an effective military leader, he found his personality cold. On the other's side, Eisenhower thought WSC's faith in the Anglo-American alliance as a catch-all solution to global political problems was over-simplistic. In December 1953 WSC persuaded Eisenhower to attend a conference at Bermuda (he believed the golf courses there would keep the President content). It was the first post-war summit between the American and British leaders. Also joining them was the Prime Minister of France, Joseph Laniel, whose attendance WSC had not been too keen on. Indeed, on the jet-ride over the Atlantic WSC was reading a novel by C. S. Forester set during the Napoleonic Wars called *Death to the*

French. At the talks WSC could not persuade Eisenhower to see the distinction between conventional weapons and the nuclear bomb. WSC saw the latter as something that could bring doom to humanity, whereas he believed Eisenhower merely viewed it as a bigger weapon. He also could not persuade Eisenhower to commit the USA to defending the Suez Canal if necessary (this would prove crucial during the Suez Crisis of 1956).

STEPPING DOWN

Following a series of strokes, WSC resigned as Prime Minister in April 1955, stepping down in favour of the Foreign Secretary Anthony Eden. WSC and Clemmie held a small farewell dinner at 10 Downing Street to mark the occasion. The only guests were Anne Chamberlain (Neville's widow), Elizabeth II and Prince Philip. At the dinner WSC wore the full court dress of black knee-breeches with his Order of the Garter and various medals and awards.

CHAPTER 10

At Home With Winston

✌ Pussie and Pug

WSC and Clemmie's pet names for each other were 'pug' (or 'pig') and 'pussie', respectively. They often greeted each other with animal noises, with WSC woofing and Clemmie miaowing. When WSC wrote to Clemmie he frequently adorned his signature with doodles of pugs or pigs.

THE FIRST CHILD

Both WSC and Clemmie had experienced a fairly distant relationship with their parents, and they were determined to be active and loving with their own children. Ten months after their marriage, WSC and Clemmie's first child, Diana, was born on 11 July 1909 at their London house on Eccleston Square. Diana spent some time at RADA and in December 1932 at the age of twenty-three married John Milner Bailey, the son of a South African diamond tycoon. This marriage ended in divorce after less than three years.

In September 1935 Diana married Duncan Sandys, a former diplomat and Conservative MP; they had three children. Sandys became a close political ally of WSC, and like him was critical of the Chamberlain ministry's appeasement policies and lack of military preparedness. A member of the Territorial Army, Sandys served in the Norwegian campaign. In 1941 he suffered a serious car accident in Wales, which led to severe leg injuries that left him with a life-long limp. Although Sandys lost his seat in Parliament in 1945, he returned as an MP in 1950 and served in several cabinet positions. In the Second World War, Diana had served in the Women's Royal Naval Service. She divorced from Sandys in 1960 and struggled afterwards with depression and nervous breakdowns; tragically, she committed suicide in 1963 following an overdose of barbiturates.

WINSTON THE FIREMAN

In August 1908 WSC was staying with his cousins Freddie and Henry Guest at Burley-on-the-Hill House, a seventeenth-century mansion in Rutland they had rented out. At 1 a.m. a fire broke out following a party. The guests fled the house. Eddie Marsh, WSC's private secretary, lost all of his luggage, including the cabinet papers he was carrying for his boss. WSC rushed back in to save rare books and artwork, and when the fire brigade arrived he was found clambering out of the mansion carrying marble busts. At the time, Clemmie and WSC were in their early courtship and corresponding constantly. When Clemmie, who was staying in the Isle of Wight, heard of the fire she telegraphed WSC to make sure he was safe. He wrote back to say he was. Less than a week later, WSC and Clemmie were engaged.

CHURCHILL'S HEIR?

WSC and Clemmie only had one son: Randolph, born on 28 May 1911 (two weeks late) at Eccleston Square in London. Before his birth WSC had nicknamed him the 'Chum Bolly' (the sobriquet either arose from a flower native to north-west India or from the Farsi word for a healthy, new-born baby). WSC was determined to be more supportive to his son than his father had been to him. He was hugely encouraging to Randolph, although he did tend to spoil him. Randolph attended Eton and then started at Oxford in 1929 after Lindemann helped to secure him a place. He spent much of his time drinking and socializing and dropped out after less than two years to go on a speaking tour of the USA. He then worked as a journalist, but had to be financially bailed out after losing money betting on the 1931 General Election (as a condition of this, WSC made him give up his Bentley).

Randolph sought a political career, and in February 1935 stood as an independent candidate at the Liverpool Wavertree by-election. His platform was based on re-armament and opposition to Indian Home Rule. His candidacy split the Conservative vote and contributed to the Labour candidate winning victory. The next month Randolph supported an independent conservative candidate (Richard Findlay, who was also a member of the British Union of Fascists) in the Norwood by-election. Rather awkwardly, he had run against the official Conservative candidate, Duncan Sandys, who became Randolph's brother-in-law later that year. Randolph stood for election to Parliament in November 1935 and February 1936, but lost both times.

When the Second World War started in 1939 Randolph joined the Fourth Hussars, his father's old regiment. He was part of the delegation sent to pick up the Duke and Duchess of Windsor from France, where they had been exiled since Edward had abdicated. As this was a formal occasion, Randolph wore his full dress uniform, which included spurs. The duke noticed that Randolph had attached the spurs upside-down and bent over to correct them. He spent the voyage from Cherbourg to Portsmouth repeatedly teasing Randolph. In late September Randolph met Pamela

Digby, an English aristocrat and socialite who was working at the Foreign Office. He proposed the night they met and they were married on 4 October (their only son, named Winston, was born a year later – he went on to become a Conservative MP and died in 2010).

In September 1940 Randolph finally became an MP, winning the Preston by-election after running unopposed. However, he continued his military career – after transferring to the British Commandos he served in North Africa and was part of the special operations unit that parachuted into Yugoslavia to link up with Tito's partisans. By this time his marriage was breaking down. Pamela had numerous affairs, including with the American diplomat W. Averell Harriman, and they divorced on grounds of desertion in 1946. Pamela went on to be romantically involved with many influential men, including the American publisher Jock Whitney, Prince Aly Khan (father of the Aga Khan), Gianni Agnelli (a scion of the wealthy Italian family that owns Fiat) and the banker Baron Élie de Rothschild. In 1960 she married the Broadway producer Leland Hayward and emigrated to New York. After Hayward died in 1971 she married her old flame Harriman. Pamela became an active and successful fund-raiser for the Democratic Party, and Bill Clinton appointed her to be the US Ambassador to France, in which position she served from 1993 to 1995. She died in 1997 in Paris.

Randolph's post-war career in politics was unsuccessful. He lost his parliamentary seat in 1945, drunk heavily, behaved obnoxiously in public and frequently argued with his father. In November 1948 he married June Osborne (they divorced in 1961). Their only daughter, Arabella, became a Buddhist and charity fund-raiser and was involved in the creation of the Glastonbury Festival; she died in 2007. During the 1950s, Randolph made several attempts to become an MP again, losing twice in parliamentary elections in Plymouth (his opponent was the future Labour Party leader Michael Foot) and failing to be selected as the Conservative candidate for Bournemouth. He then made a successful return to journalism and writing, and oversaw the first stages of his father's official biography. Randolph was not able to complete the work because he died of a heart attack, following years of heavy drinking and smoking, in 1968.

'THE MULE'

On 7 October 1914 Sarah Churchill was born at Admiralty House. She was a striking child – witty and with bright red hair – though WSC came to nickname her affectionately 'the mule' because of her stubbornness. She studied ballet and became a dancer and actress, making her stage debut aged twenty-one as a chorus girl at the Adelphi Theatre in London. She became romantically involved with Vic Oliver, an Austrian-born actor and comedian over sixteen years her senior. Oliver was a West End star and a popular fixture on BBC broadcasts (he was the first ever guest on *Desert Island Discs*). Despite her parents' disapproval they married in 1936 in New York (WSC had sent his son Randolph across the Atlantic to try and stop the wedding), but they divorced in 1945. After the Second World War broke out, Sarah joined the Women's Auxiliary Air Force, working as an intelligence analyst of surveillance photographs. She also served as her father's aide, accompanying him on numerous foreign trips, including to the Tehran and Yalta conferences.

After the war Sarah resumed her acting career, appearing in several films, television programmes and theatrical productions. Her most famous role was in the 1951 musical comedy *Royal Wedding*, where she played opposite Fred Astaire. Sarah married for the second time in 1949, to an American photographer called Anthony Beauchamp. Her parents were not introduced to the man and were not informed of the wedding. Beauchamp died after an overdose of sleeping pills in 1957. Her third and final marriage was in 1962, to Thomas Touchet-Jesson, twenty-third Baron Audley. In Audley she had finally found a partner her parents approved of who brought her real happiness, but he sadly died in 1963. Sarah faced a long-term struggle with drinking, and frequently ran into trouble with the police for disturbing the peace. She carried on acting until 1971, before turning to poetry and painting; after a long illness, she died in 1982.

✌ A Country Retreat

After leaving the Admiralty, WSC needed somewhere to contemplate his future. In summer 1915, together with his brother Jack, he rented a property near Godalming in Surrey as a weekend retreat for them and their families. Hoe Farm was a sixteenth-century farmhouse that had been extended by the famed architect Sir Edwin Lutyens (who coincidentally was the brother-in-law of WSC's first great love Pamela Plowden). It was at Hoe Farm that WSC first painted, a hobby that would stay with him for the rest of his life.

LULLENDEN

In spring 1917 WSC purchased a Tudor farmhouse called Lullenden, near East Grinstead. It cost £6,000 (over £300,000 today) but had many structural problems. As London was subject to bombing from German zeppelins, Clemmie and the children spent most of their time at Lullenden while WSC worked in the capital. The children went to a school in the village of Dormansland, travelling there by pony and trap. In late 1919 the Churchills' money troubles meant they had to sell Lullenden. Fortunately, their friends Sir Ian and Lady Jean Hamilton had fallen in love with the place and bought it for the price of £10,000 (which helped finance the purchase of the London property at Sussex Square).

MARIGOLD

The fourth Churchill child, Marigold, was born at 3 Tenterden Street, the Churchill's rented house in London, on 15 November 1918, four days after the First World War ended. WSC nicknamed her the 'Duckadilly'. Tragically, her life was brief. In 1921 WSC had rented his family a cottage at Broadstairs, on the Kentish coast. That summer WSC had to travel north to Scotland while Clemmie had taken a trip to Cheshire to visit the Duke of Westminster. Marigold was left in the care of her French nanny, Mademoiselle Rose. When Marigold came down with a cold, Rose did not notify her parents until it had developed into a serious infection. WSC and Clemmie returned to Kent in time to be by Marigold's side when she died on 23 August. Both parents were distraught.

A TIMELY INHERITANCE

Between 1848 and 1856 Frances Vane, Marchioness of Londonderry (she was WSC's great-grandmother; her daughter married the seventh Duke of Marlborough) built a summer residence near Carnlough in County Antrim. The cliff-top castle was called Garron Tower, and it and its surrounding land were to prove extremely useful to WSC.

By 1921 the Garron Tower estate had been inherited by the Marchioness of Londonderry's grandson Lord Herbert Vane-Tempest. He was the chairman of Cambrian Railways, but died in a tragic train collision at Abermule that killed sixteen others. As Lord Herbert was childless, Garron Tower (and some jewellery) was inherited by his first cousin once removed, WSC. It gave him an annual income of £4,000 from ground rents and helped to shore up his finances. Although Clemmie warned WSC to be cautious with this windfall, part of the bequest went towards the purchase of Chartwell the next year. WSC also used Garron Tower as a security for mortgages and put it towards his children's trust funds. He visited his Irish estate just once, in 1926, but only for one day, and had sold it by the 1930s. Garron Tower itself became a hotel until 1939, housed evacuees during the Second World War and since 1951 has been a school.

CHARTWELL

A fter the sale of Lullenden, WSC was on the hunt for a country house. In July 1921 he viewed a property near Westerham in Kent: Chartwell. The house was undistinguished; it was a sprawling red-brick mansion enlarged from a Tudor farmhouse and needed considerable restoration work. It was the views over the Weald of Kent that enraptured WSC. Clemmie was less enthusiastic; she did not want to commit the family's finances to such a large and potentially expensive property. WSC's desires ultimately prevailed. After Chartwell failed to sell at auction, its owner, Captain Archibald John Campbell Colquhoun, offered it to WSC (who he had known at Harrow) for £5,500. Due to the house's poor state WSC offered £4,800. They eventually settled on £5,000 (over £250,000 today), and the sale was completed in November 1922.

WSC wanted to make extensive changes to Chartwell; he aimed to re-orientate the house so it could better enjoy the views over the countryside. He hired Philip Tilden, a society architect who had done work for his friends David Lloyd George and Sir Philip Sassoon. The rebuilding work cost over £15,000, and there were frequent disputes between Tilden and WSC. Delays in construction, primarily due to damp, meant that WSC could not actually stay at Chartwell until April 1924. The house became his most treasured retreat and the headquarters of his literary enterprises.

Chartwell was not cheap to run – in the 1920s the annual wage bill was £2,000, which covered two kitchen servants, two pantry servants, two housemaids, a lady's maid, a nursemaid, a nanny, an 'odd man' for miscellaneous work, two secretaries, a chauffeur, a groom and a bailiff (to save money they did not employ a trained cook). Money troubles meant WSC often faced the prospect of having to sell Chartwell. Losses in the stock market in 1929 forced him to dust-sheet most of the house, leaving only his study open. Likewise, share losses and mounting debts in 1938 left WSC on a precipice. Happily for him and his family, a combination of income from writing and timely financial help from well-wishers like Bernard Baruch and Henry Strakosch meant he never had to sell the house.

During the Second World War, Chartwell mostly stood empty; its proximity to France meant it was exposed to German bombing raids. WSC could only pay occasional, brief visits. After the war ended, WSC considered putting Chartwell up for sale due to the costs of running it. His friend William Berry, Viscount Camrose, owner of the *Daily Telegraph*, led a campaign to keep WSC in Chartwell while also preserving it for the public. Camrose and ten other wealthy people together donated £85,000. Chartwell was purchased from WSC for £50,000 with the proviso that he and Clemmie could remain there for the rest of their lives. The remaining £35,000 of the fund went towards an endowment to the National Trust, who would take over management of the property after the Churchills left. Although Clemmie had the right to stay there, she left Chartwell in June 1965, and the property opened to the public in 1966.

✌ Honoured Guests

Chartwell welcomed hundreds of guests over the years. The visitors' book lists 780 names, including Arthur Balfour, Anthony Eden, Ted Heath, Vivien Leigh, David Lloyd George,

T. E. Lawrence, Harold Macmillan, Sir Laurence Olivier and Harry S. Truman. Aside from direct family the most frequent guests were Frederick Lindemann (86 visits), Clemmie's cousin Sylvia Henley (85), Field Marshal Bernard Montgomery (46), Brendan Bracken (31) and WSC's last private secretary Anthony Montague Browne (24).

THE YOUNGEST CHURCHILL

Mary Churchill was born in London on 15 September 1922, just over a year after the death of Marigold. She had a very stable childhood, spending most of it at Chartwell. Mary was blessed with a loving nanny, 'Nana' Maryott Whyte, who oversaw her early years in the idyllic countryside and estate that surrounded Chartwell. Due to WSC's political 'exile' in the 1930s, Mary was able to spend a lot of time with her father as she grew up.

Like her siblings she entered the armed forces during the Second World War, joining the Auxiliary Territorial Service (the women's branch of the British Army) in 1941. She helped to operate anti-aircraft batteries, rising to the rank of junior commander, and serving in Belgium after D-Day. She also joined her father on overseas trips, such as to the Potsdam Conference. After the war Mary devoted herself to charity and public service, as well as writing a biography of her mother and several other books. In 2005 Mary followed in her father's footsteps by being invested into the Order of the Garter.

On 11 February 1947 Mary married Christopher Soames, an officer in the Coldstream Guards she had met in Paris. The wedding took place at St Margaret's Westminster, where WSC and Clemmie had married. Soames became a Conservative MP and served as the last British Governor of Southern Rhodesia (now Zimbabwe) from 1979 to 1980. After Mary's marriage, she and Christopher moved into Chartwell Farm, near to the main house, where they lived for ten years. WSC was closer to Christopher than to his other children-in-law; they both had an interest in racehorses and enjoyed playing gin rummy together. The Soames had five children and remained married until Christopher's death in 1987. Mary died in 2014.

CHURCHILL'S BANKS

WSC first banked with Cox's of Pall Mall. The firm was founded in 1758 for the First Regiment of Foot Guards and over the years expanded to become the main banker to soldiers in the British Army. In 1922 Cox's merged with another firm, Henry S. King; it was then acquired by Lloyds Bank the next year. WSC was not always the most reliable customer; he frequently wrote cheques he did not have the funds for but trusted that the bank would honour based on his status and reputation. Due to his American financial holdings, WSC also banked with National City Bank of New York (now known as Citibank). He often engaged in short-term currency speculation using his American bank, cabling them with the codeword 'WINCH' when he wanted them to make a purchase.

✌ Panda Place-Holder

To ensure that books in Chartwell's library were returned to their correct locations on the shelves, WSC would use a stuffed toy panda to mark their place when they were taken down.

THE SUSPECTED AFFAIRS

....

The marriages of both Clemmie and WSC's parents had been beset by affairs. In comparison, their own union was remarkably stable despite the stresses of WSC's political career, losing children and financial difficulties. There have been rumours of infidelity, but they have never been fully substantiated. From December 1934 to April 1935, Clemmie went on a yachting holiday (without WSC) through South-East Asia and the Pacific as the guest of Lord Moyne, the heir to the Guinness brewing fortune. On the trip she flirted with Terence Philip, a wealthy art dealer, but there is no proof of an actual affair. Clemmie did, though, bring back a Bali dove as a gift from him, which was ultimately buried under a sun-dial at Chartwell.

There have been rumours that WSC had an affair with the socialite Lady Doris Castlerosse (the great-aunt of the model and actress Cara Delevingne). At various times between 1933 and 1937 WSC and Castlerosse holidayed together at the Château de l'Horizon at Golfe-Juan, a villa in the south of France owned by an American actress and businesswoman Maxine Elliott. WSC had painted two portraits of Castlerosse, and she had kept one. By 1942 she was living in New York, and it is said that WSC wanted to ensure that the portrait was not released to the press, as it would lead to rumours that would undermine his reputation. To prevent this, WSC, with FDR's help, arranged for Castlerosse to return to England by seaplane. She died of an overdose of sleeping pills at the Dorchester Hotel later that year. WSC's friend Lord Beaverbrook then took possession of the painting from her brother. The veracity of these rumours of WSC's supposed affair is at best doubtful; they are solely based on recordings of interviews with Jock Colville, a senior civil servant who was one of WSC's private secretaries while he was Prime Minister, made in 1985. However, Colville did not know when the affair was supposed to have taken place.

A LENGTHY BAGGAGE TRAIN

After the Second World War WSC frequently spent large parts of the year on holiday. These trips were partly to enjoy the sunshine but were also financially beneficial; they allowed him to spend his American earnings abroad without having to worry about it being taxed or about breaking British laws that limited the amount of currency that could be exported. WSC tended to travel with a large entourage of staff, family members and friends; it was not rare for them to have over a hundred items of luggage between them. Clemmie tended not to accompany WSC on his foreign trips in the 1950s and 60s because she was unwell with neuritis and preferred to stay at home.

HONOURS

WSC received honours from countries across the world, including Estonia (Cross of Liberty), Belgium (Grand Cordon of the Order of Leopold), the Netherlands (Knight Grand Cross of the Order of the Netherlands Lion), Norway (Grand Cross with Collar, Royal Norwegian Order of St Olav), Denmark (Knight of the Order of the Elephant), Nepal (Most Refulgent Order of the Star of Nepal), Libya (Grand Sash of the High Order of Sayyid Muhammad ibn Ali as-Senussi) and the Czech Republic (Order of the White Lion, awarded posthumously).

His most prestigious award was being made a Knight of the Garter. This is the oldest and most prestigious chivalric order in Britain, consisting of the monarch and twenty-four knights they personally choose. In 1945 WSC had turned down George VI when offered the honour because at the time he had just been voted out of office and did not think it was appropriate to accept. When Elizabeth II again offered WSC the chance to become a Knight of the Garter in 1953 he accepted. However, he refused the highly prestigious honour of being made the Duke of London in 1955, because he was worried it would interfere with his son Randolph's political career (at this stage he was still seeking to become an MP). The duchy would have been hereditary, and it meant that under British law at that time, when WSC died Randolph would have automatically become a member of the House of Lords.

Clemmie was also honoured; in 1946 she was made a Dame Grand Cross of the Order of the British Empire. Four months after WSC died, she was made a life peer and given the title Baroness Spencer-Churchill of Chartwell. She sat in the House of Lords as an independent cross-bencher, but due to hearing problems she became unable to attend regularly. However, in 1973 she was well enough to unveil yet another honour for her husband; his official statue, sculpted by Ivor Roberts-Jones, which stands in Parliament Square.

✌ The Churchill Coin

After WSC died in 1965, the Royal Mint commemorated his life by portraying him on a crown (worth five shillings, or approximately £5 in today's money); he was the first non-royal to appear on a British coin.

LAST ILLNESSES

In his later years WSC became increasingly frail. In 1960 he suffered a fall and broke a small bone in his neck. Two years later he fell out of bed while staying in his penthouse at the Hôtel de Paris in Monte Carlo and broke his hip. He lay on the floor for an hour before his nurses found him. He was flown to England on a De Havilland Comet, landing at RAF Northolt and being taken to Middlesex Hospital in London to recuperate. As a result of his injury, lifts had to be installed at his London home. WSC was also growing deaf but refused to wear a hearing aid. Despite his ailing health he continued to attend Parliament periodically, visiting the House of Commons for the last time on 27 July 1964. WSC's poor health meant he had to leave his beloved Chartwell for the last time in mid-October that year. He spent his last days at Hyde Park Gate, appearing at his window on his ninetieth birthday to make his famous V-for-Victory sign to the crowds that assembled outside.

THE FUNERAL

When WSC died on 24 January 1965 (the seventieth anniversary of his father's passing), following a severe stroke, he had been in a coma for several days. Detailed plans for his funeral were first drawn up in 1958; they were known privately in the Cabinet Office as 'Operation Hope Not'. Bernard Fitzalan-Howard, Duke of Norfolk, in his hereditary role as Earl Marshal (who oversees the most important ceremonial state occasions), modelled his plans on the state funerals of the likes of Nelson, Pitt the Younger, Wellington and Gladstone. They went through eight revisions because the projected pall-bearers kept passing away; the ones eventually selected were:

- Harold Macmillan, Prime Minister 1957–63

- Field Marshal Sir Gerald Templer, commander of British and Commonwealth forces in the Malayan Emergency

- Edward Bridges, Baron Bridges, WSC's Cabinet Secretary during the Second World War

- Field Marshal William Slim, Viscount Slim, who led Allied Forces in Burma in the Second World War

- Anthony Eden, Earl of Avon, Prime Minister 1955–7

- Field Marshal Harold Alexander, Earl Alexander of Tunis, who commanded Allied armies in Burma, North Africa and Italy

- Sir Robert Menzies, Prime Minister of Australia 1939–41 and 1949–66

- Norman Brook, Baron Normanbrook, Cabinet Secretary 1947–62

- Hastings Ismay, Baron Ismay, WSC's senior military assistant in the Second World War and first Secretary General of NATO

- Marshal of the RAF, Charles Portal, Viscount Portal of Hungerford, Chief of the Air Staff during the Second World War

- Clement Attlee, Earl Attlee, Prime Minister 1945–51

- Admiral of the Fleet, Louis Mountbatten, Earl Mountbatten of Burma, the last Viceroy of India

WSC lay in state at Westminster Hall from 27 to 30 January; over 300,000 filed past his coffin. There followed a procession (that passed by St Margaret's Westminster, where he had married Clemmie) to St Paul's Cathedral, where the funeral service was held. Officials from over a hundred countries attended. After being carried to the Tower of London and taken across the Thames on a launch called the MV *Havengore*, the coffin was subsequently conveyed by train from Waterloo to Hanborough Station in Oxfordshire, and carried to St Martin's Church in Bladon, where WSC was buried following a private family ceremony. The churchyard there also includes the graves of WSC's parents, brother, wife and children (with the exception of Marigold, who was buried in Kensal Green Cemetery).

Selected Bibliography

Best, Geoffrey, *Churchill: A Study in Greatness* (London and New York: Hambledon, 2001)

Bonham Carter, Violet, *Churchill As I Knew Him* (London: Pan, 1967)

Churchill, Winston S., *The Story of the Malakand Field Force* (London: Longmans, 1898)

Churchill, Winston S., *My African Journey* (London: Hodder & Stoughton, 1908)

Churchill, Winston S., *The River War* (London: Eyre & Spottiswoode, 1951)

Churchill, Winston S., *My Early Life: A Roving Commission* (London: Collins, 1969)

Churchill, Winston S., *The Boer War: London to Ladysmith via Pretoria and Ian Hamilton's March* (London: Bloomsbury, 2013)

Clarke, Peter, *Mr Churchill's Profession: Statesman, Orator, Writer* (London: Bloomsbury, 2012)

Colville, John, *The Churchillians* (London: Weidenfeld & Nicolson, 1981)

Coughlin, Con, *Churchill's First War: Young Winston and the Fight Against the Taliban* (Basingstoke: Macmillan, 2013)

D'Este, Carlo, *Warlord: A Life of Churchill at War, 1874–1945* (London: Allen Lane, 2009)

Dewar Gibb, Andrew, *With Winston Churchill at the Front* (London and Glasgow: Gowans and Gray, 1924)

Dobbs, Michael, *Six Months in 1945: FDR, Stalin, Churchill, and Truman – From World War to Cold War* (London: Arrow, 2013)

Edmonds, Robin, *The Big Three: Churchill, Roosevelt and Stalin in Peace & War* (London: Hamish Hamilton, 1991)

Farmelo, Graham, *Churchill's Bomb: A Hidden History of Science, War and Politics* (London: Faber & Faber, 2013)

Gilbert, Martin, *Churchill: A Life* (London: Heinemann, 1991)

Gilbert, Martin, *In Search of Churchill: A Historian's Journey* (London: HarperCollins, 1994)

Gilbert, Martin, ed., *Churchill: The Power of Words* (London: Bantam, 2012)

Haldane, Aylmer, *How We Escaped From Pretoria* (Edinburgh and London: W. Blackwood, 1901)

James, Lawrence, *Churchill and Empire* (London: Phoenix, 2014)

Jenkins, Roy, *Churchill* (London: Macmillan, 2001)

Johnson, Boris, *The Churchill Factor: How One Man Made History* (London: Hodder & Stoughton, 2014)

Lee, Celia and Lee, John, *The Churchills: A Family Portrait* (Basingstoke: Palgrave Macmillan, 2010)

Lloyd George, Robert, *David & Winston: How a Friendship Changed History* (London: John Murray, 2005)

Lovell, Mary S., *The Churchills: A Family at the Heart of History* (New York: Little, Brown, 2011)

McCarten, Anthony, *Darkest Hour: How Churchill Brought Us Back from the Brink* (London: Penguin, 2017)

McMoran Wilson, Charles, *Winston Churchill: The Struggle for Survival, 1940–1965* (London: Sphere Books, 1968)

Paterson, Michael, *Winston Churchill: Personal Accounts of the Great Leader at War* (Cincinnati: David & Charles, 2005)

Reynolds, David, *In Command of History: Churchill Fighting and Writing the Second World War* (London: Allen Lane, 2004)

Rose, Jonathan, *The Literary Churchill: Author, Reader, Actor* (New Haven and London: Yale University Press, 2014)

Shakespeare, Nicholas, *Six Minutes in May: How Churchill Unexpectedly Became Prime Minister* (London: Harvill Secker, 2017)

Shelden, Michael, *Young Titan: The Making of Winston Churchill* (London: Simon & Schuster, 2013)

Soames, Mary, *Winston Churchill: His Life as a Painter* (London: Collins, 1990)

Stafford, David, *Churchill and Secret Service* (London: John Murray, 1997)

Stelzer, Cita, *Dinner with Churchill: Policy-Making at the Dinner Table* (London: Short Books, 2011)

Thompson, Walter H., *I Was Churchill's Shadow* (London: Christopher Johnson, 1951)

Toye, Richard, *Lloyd George & Churchill: Rivals for Greatness* (Basingstoke: Macmillan, 2007)

Wheeler-Bennett, John, ed., *Action This Day: Working with Churchill* (London: Macmillan, 1968)

Index

WSC indicates Winston Churchill.